IDLE DAYS IN PATAGONIA

AT LAST, PATAGONIA

Travellers, Explorers & Pioneers

IDLE DAYS IN PATAGONIA

W.H. HUDSON

NONSUCH

First published 1893
Copyright © in this edition 2005
Nonsuch Publishing Ltd

Nonsuch Publishing Limited
The Mill, Brimscombe Port,
Stroud, Gloucestershire, GL5 2QG
www.nonsuch-publishing.com

British Library Cataloguing in Publication Data.
A catalogue record for this book is available from the British Library.

1-84588-024-2

Typesetting and origination by Nonsuch Publishing Limited
Printed in Great Britain by Oaklands Book Services Limited

CONTENTS

INTRODUCTION TO THE
MODERN EDITION

In a corner of Hyde Park, shaded and shadowed by overhanging trees, there is a stone monument of Rima, bird-girl of the forest. Rima was the orphaned daughter of a mystical race, an ethereal and benevolent spirit. But this is not an icon of religious worship; rather, it is a simple and beautiful tribute to a writer and his works, which inspired, among others, the sculptor of this piece, Jacob Epstein. The author to whom this tribute is paid is the novelist and naturalist William Henry Hudson. His writings, from his many romances to his delicate studies of wildlife, from the Argentinean pampas of his youth to the more familiar skies of Hampshire and Cornwall, have won him countless admirers. *Idle Days in Patagonia*, a 'tranquil contemplative, work of reflection' is an account of this young adventurer's time on the Patagonian shores. As a descriptive record, it has long been held as immensely valuable; as a work of literature, it is just as finely crafted as the 'solitary wilderness' of which travellers remain in similarly gentle awe.

That Hudson should be drawn to South America should be of no surprise. He was born in 1841, to Anglo-American parents near Quilmes, in the Province of Buenos Aires. His father was a sheep farmer, though in this his fortunes were mixed. He was eventually forced to abandon his efforts, and to open a faltering grocery store, but not before his son had contracted rheumatic fever whilst herding cattle through a storm. The 'privileges of the invalid' allowed Hudson time to observe the natural world, and with it he soon developed a fascination. He painstakingly recorded the movements of the birds and animals of his homeland, and with this was born a preoccupation which was to carve for him his future.

In 1874 financial circumstances dictated that Hudson should move to London. He married an older woman who ran a boarding house of sorts.

A somewhat loveless union, it is rumoured to have been interspersed with numerous and passionate affairs. Hudson's writing had been honed by both its practise and by the tuition of the learned travellers who had stayed with his family in Argentina, but for many years he struggled in obscure poverty. He published articles and small pieces in various journals, but received no great acclaim, until, in 1892, Chapman and Hall published *The Naturalist in La Plata*. Hudson immediately became regarded as the finest nature writer of his time. This particular work is still, in fact, considered essential reading within the field.

The precise quality of his observation was matched by the engaging style of his writing, winning praise from such literary figures as Virginia Woolf in the Common Reader. He had already written at least one novel at this point, *The Purple Land*, and went on to write several more. Foremost among them is *Green Mansions* (1904), a romance set in the South American wilds, which has never since gone out of print. It is from this work that Epstein chose the figure of Rima for his sculpture.

For a character of Hudson's particular make-up, a return to Patagonia might have been written in the skies. He would have been well aware of the experiences of the French explorer Auguste Guinnard, whose factual account, *Three Years Slavery Amongst the Patagonians* (1871), had lately gripped the informed world. In the same year, George C. Musters had released his seminal work *At Home with the Patagonians*. This empathetic account of the Teheulche Indians, a work still thought of as one of the most authoritative ethnographic documents of these people, would have further fanned the flames of interest in a land that was once on Hudson's own doorstep. He could hardly but have joined their ranks, and become what the ethnographer Malinowski describes as another 'Argonaut of the Western Pacific'.

Patagonia had long inspired wonder amongst the explorers of the world. Ever since Antonia Pigafetta described meeting men of towering stature on Magellan's historic voyage, it had become, in the popular imagination, an 'ancient habitation of giants.' It is a unique land, possessed of both volcanos and glaciers, barren basalt steppes and verdant valleys. For the naturalist, it is not, however, the 'giants' which stagger the senses, but the animals that might play at their feet; the shy deer-like guanaco, the zorro or the tuco-tuco. For Hudson in particular, it was the dazzling birdlife that was the real treasure to be found. Julius Beerbohm had described the rheas (*rhea darwinii*), in the fascinating *Wanderings in Patagonia* (1879), and these creatures were only one among many of their kind. But this work is so much more than a prosaic account of wonders. *Idle Days in Patagonia* is simply a beguiling tale of how one may see the world differently, when one might take the time. And this is a fact that is also best summed-up by Hudson himself:

Our waking life is sometimes like a dream, which proceeds logically enough until the stimulus of some new sensation, from without or within, throws it into temporary confusion, or suspends its action; after which it goes on again, but with fresh characters, passions, and motives, and a changed argument.

RHINOCRYPTA LANCEOLATA

I

AT LAST, PATAGONIA!

THE wind had blown a gale all night, and I had been hourly expecting that the tumbling, storm-vexed old steamer, in which I had taken passage to the Rio Negro, would turn over once for all and settle down beneath that tremendous tumult of waters. For the groaning sound of its straining timbers, and the engine throbbing like an over-tasked human heart, had made the ship seem a living thing to me; and it was tired of the struggle, and under the tumult was peace. But at about three o'clock in the morning the wind began to moderate, and, taking off coat and boots, I threw myself into my bunk for a little sleep.

Ours, it must be said, was a very curious boat, reported ancient and much damaged; long and narrow in shape, like a Viking's ship, with the passengers' cabins ranged like a row of small cottages on the deck: it was as ugly to look at as it was said to be unsafe to voyage in. To make matters worse our captain, a man over eighty years old, was lying in his cabin sick unto death, for, as a fact, he died not many days after our mishap; our one mate was asleep, leaving only the men to navigate the steamer on that perilous coast, and in the darkest hour of a tempestuous night.

I was just dropping into a doze when a succession of bumps, accompanied by strange grating and grinding noises, and shuddering motions of the ship, caused me to start up again and rush to the cabin door. The night was still black and starless, with wind and rain, but for acres round us the sea was whiter than milk. I did not step out; close to me, half-way between my cabin door and the bulwarks, where our only boat was fastened, three of the sailors were standing together talking in low tones. "We are lost," I heard one say; and another answer, "Ay, lost for ever!" Just then the mate, roused from sleep, came running to them. "Good God, what have you done with the steamer!" he exclaimed sharply; then, dropping his voice, he added, "Lower the boat—quick!"

I crept out and stood, unseen by them in the obscurity, within five feet of the group. Not a thought of the dastardly character of the act they were about to engage in—for it was their intention to save themselves and leave us to our fate—entered my mind at the time. My only thought was that at the last moment, when they would be unable to prevent it except by knocking me senseless, I would spring with them into the boat and save myself, or else perish with them in that awful white surf. But one other person, more experienced than myself, and whose courage took another and better form, was also near and listening. He was the first engineer—a young Englishman from Newcastle-on-Tyne. Seeing the men making for the boat, he slipped out of the engine-room, revolver in hand and secretly followed them; and when the mate gave that order, he stepped forward with the weapon raised, and said in a quiet but determined voice that he would shoot the first man who should attempt to obey it. The men slunk away and disappeared in the gloom. In a few moments more the passengers began streaming out on to the deck in a great state of alarm; last of all the old captain, white and hollow-eyed from his death-bed, appeared like a ghost among us. He had not been long standing there, with arms folded on his chest, issuing no word of command, and paying no attention to the agitated questions addressed to him by the passengers, when, by some lucky chance, the steamer got off the rocks and plunged on for a space through the seething, milky surf; then, very suddenly, passed out of it into black and comparatively calm water. For ten or twelve minutes she sped rapidly and smoothly on; then it was said that she had ceased to move, that we were stuck fast in the sand of the shore, although no shore was visible in the intense darkness, and to me it seemed that we were still moving swiftly on.

There was no longer any wind, and through the now fast-breaking clouds ahead of us appeared the first welcome signs of dawn. By degrees the darkness grew less intense; only just ahead of us there still remained something black and unchangeable—a portion, as it were, of that pitchy gloom that a short time before had made sea and air appear one and indistinguishable; but as the light increased it changed not, and at last it was seen to be a range of low hills or dunes of sand scarcely a stone's throw from the ship's bows. It was true enough that we were stuck fast in the sand; and although this was a safer bed for the steamer than the jagged rocks, the position was still a perilous one, and I at once determined to land. Three other passengers resolved to bear me company; and as the tide had now gone out, and the water at the bows was barely waist deep, we were lowered by means of ropes into the sea, and quickly waded to the shore.

We were not long in scrambling up the dunes to get a sight of the country beyond. At last, Patagonia! How often had I pictured in imagination, wishing with an intense longing to visit this solitary wilderness, resting far off in its primitive and desolate peace, untouched by man, remote from civilization! There it lay full in sight before me—the unmarred desert that wakes strange feelings in us; the ancient habitation of giants, whose footprints seen on the sea-shore amazed

OUR CAPTAIN

Magellan and his men, and won for it the name of Patagonia. There, too, far away in the interior, was the place called Trapalanda, and the spirit-guarded lake, on whose margin rose the battlements of that mysterious city, which many have sought and none have found.

It was not, however, the fascination of old legends that drew me, nor the desire of the desert, for not until I had seen it, and had tasted its flavour, then, and on many subsequent occasions, did I know how much its solitude and desolation would be to me, what strange knowledge it would teach, and how enduring its effect would be on my spirit. Not these things, but the passion of the ornithologist took me. Many of the winged wanderers with which I had been familiar from childhood in La Plata were visitors, occasional or regular, from this grey wilderness of thorns. In some cases they were passengers, seen only, when they stooped to rest their wings, or heard far off "wailing their way from cloud to cloud," impelled by that mysterious thought-baffling faculty so unlike all other phenomena in its manifestations as to give it among natural things something of the supernatural. Some of these wanderers, more especially such as possess only a partial or limited migration, I hoped to meet again in Patagonia, singing their summer songs, and breeding in their summer haunts. It was also my hope to find some new species, some bird as beautiful, let us say, as the wryneck or wheatear, and as old on the earth, but which had never been named and never even seen by any appreciative human eye. I do not know how it is with other ornithologists at the time when their enthusiasm is greatest; of myself I can say that my dreams by night were often of some new bird, vividly seen; and such dreams were always beautiful to me, and a grief to wake from; yet the dream-bird often as not appeared in a modest grey colouring, or plain brown, or some other equally sober tint.

From the summit of the sandy ridge we saw before us an undulating plain, bounded only by the horizon, carpeted with short grass, seared by the summer suns, and sparsely dotted over with a few sombre-leafed bushes. It was a desert that had been a desert always, and for that very reason sweet beyond all scenes to look upon, its ancient quiet broken only by the occasional call or twitter of some small bird, while the morning air I inhaled was made delicious with a faint familiar perfume. Casting my eyes down I perceived, growing in the sand at my feet, an evening primrose plant, with at least a score of open blossoms on its low wide-spreading branches; and this, my favourite flower, both in gardens and growing wild, was the sweet perfumer of the wilderness! Its subtle fragrance, first and last, has been much to me, and has followed me from the New World to the Old, to serve sometimes as a kind of second more faithful memory, and to set my brains working on a pretty problem, to which I shall devote a chapter at the end of this book.

Our survey concluded, we set out in the direction of the Rio Negro. Before quitting the steamer the captain had spoken a few words to us. Looking at us as though he saw us not, he said that the ship had gone ashore somewhere north of the Rio Negro, about thirty miles he thought, and that we should doubtless find some herdsmen's huts on our way thither. No need then to burden ourselves with food and drink! At first we kept close to the dunes that bordered the seashore, wading through a luxuriant growth of wild liquorice—a pretty plant about eighteen inches high, with deep green feathery foliage crowned with spikes of pale blue flowers. Some of the roots which we pulled up from the loose sandy soil were over nine feet in length. All the apothecaries in the world might have laid in a few years' supply of the drug from the plants we saw on that morning.

To my mind there is nothing in life so delightful as that feeling of relief, of escape, and absolute freedom which one experiences in a vast solitude, where man has perhaps never been, and has, at any rate, left no trace of his existence. It was strong and exhilarating in me on that morning; and I was therefore by no means elated when we descried, some distance ahead, the low walls of half a dozen mud cabins. My fellow-travellers were, however, delighted at the discovery, and we hastened on, thinking that we were nearer to the settlement than we had supposed. But we found the huts uninhabited, the doors broken down, the wells choked up and overgrown with wild liquorice plants.

We learnt subsequently that a few venturesome herdsmen had made their home in this remote spot with their families, and that about a year before our visit the Indians had swept down on them and destroyed the young settlement. Very soon we turned our backs on the ruined hovels, my companions loudly expressing their disappointment, while I felt secretly glad that we were yet to drink a little more deeply of the cup of wild nature.

After walking on some distance we found a narrow path leading away southward from the ruined village, and, believing that it led direct to the Carmen, the old settlement on the Rio Negro, which is over twenty miles from the sea, we at once resolved to follow it. This path led us wide of the ocean. Before noon we lost sight of the low sand-hills on our right hand, and as we penetrated further into the interior the dark-leafed bushes I have mentioned were more abundant. The dense, stiff, dark-coloured foliage of these bushes give them a strange appearance on the pale sun-dried plains, as of black rocks of numberless fantastic forms scattered over the greyish-yellow ground. No large fowls were seen; small birds were, however, very abundant, gladdening the parched wilderness with their minstrelsy. Most noteworthy among the true songsters were the Patagonian mocking-bird and four or five finches, two of them new to me. Here I first made the acquaintance of a singular and very pretty bird—the red-breasted plant-cutter, a finch too, but only in appearance. It is a sedentary bird and sits conspicuously on the topmost twig, displaying its ruddy under plumage; occasionally emitting, by way of song, notes that resemble the faint bleatings of a kid, and, when disturbed, passing from bush to bush by a series of jerks, the wings producing a loud humming sound. Most numerous, and surpassing all others in interest, were the omnipresent dendrocolaptine bird, or wood-hewers, or tree creepers as they are sometimes called—feeble flyers, in uniform sober brown plumage; restless in their habits and loquacious, with shrill and piercing, or clear resonant voices. One terrestrial species, with a sandy-brown plumage, *Upucerthia dumetoria*, raced along before us on the ground, in appearance a stout miniature ibis with very short legs and exaggerated beak. Every bush had its little colony of brown gleaners, small birds of the genus *Synallaxis*, moving restlessly about among the leaves, occasionally suspending themselves from the twigs head downwards, after the manner of tits. From the distance at intervals came the piercing cries of the cachalote (*Homorus gutturalis*) a much larger bird, sounding like bursts of hysterical laughter. All these dendrocolaptine birds have an inordinate passion for building, and their nests are very much larger than small birds usually make. Where they are abundant the trees and bushes are sometimes laden with their enormous fabrics, so that the thought is forced on one that these busy little architects do assuredly occupy themselves with a vain unprofitable labour. It is not only the case that many a small bird builds a nest as big as a buzzard's, only to contain half a dozen eggs the size of peas, which might very comfortably be hatched in a pill-box; but frequently, when the nest has been finished, the builder sets about demolishing it to get the materials for constructing a second nest. One very common species, *Anumbius acuticaudatus*, variously called in the vernacular the thorn-bird, the woodman, and the firewood-gatherer, sometimes makes three nests in the course of a year, each composed of a good armful of sticks. The woodman's nest is, however, an insignificant structure compared with that of the obstreperous cachalote mentioned a moment ago. This bird, which is about as large as a missel thrush, selects a low thorny bush with stout wide-spreading branches, and in the centre of it builds a domed nest of sticks, perfectly spherical and four or five feet deep. The opening is at the side near the top, and leading to it there is a narrow arched gallery resting on a horizontal branch, and about fourteen inches long. So compactly made is this enormous nest that I have found it hard to break one up. I have also stood upright on the dome and stamped on it with my boots without injuring it at all. During my stay in Patagonia I found about a dozen of these palatial nests; and my opinion is that like our own houses, or, rather, our public buildings, and some ant-hills, and the vizcacha's village burrows, and the beaver's dam, it is made to last for ever.

The only mammal we saw was a small armadillo, *Dasypus minutus*; it was quite common, and early in the day, when we were still fresh and full of spirits, we amused ourselves by chasing them. We captured several, and one of my companions, an Italian, killed two and slung them over his shoulder, remarking that we could cook and eat them if we grew hungry before reaching our destination. We were not much troubled with hunger, but towards noon we began to suffer somewhat from thirst. At midday we saw before us a low level plain, covered with long coarse grass of a dull yellowish-green colour. Here we hoped to find water, and before long we descried the white gleam of a lagoon, as we imagined, but on a nearer inspection the white appearance of water turned out to be only a salt efflorescence on a barren patch of ground. On this plain it was excessively sultry; not a bush could be found to shelter us from the sun: all was a monotonous desert of coarse yellowish grass, out of which rose, as we advanced, multitudes of mosquitoes, trumpeting a shrill derisive welcome. The glory of the morning that had so enchanted us at the outset had died out of nature, and the scene was almost hateful to look on. We were getting tired, too, but the heat and our thirst, and the intolerable *fi fo fum* of the ravenous mosquitoes would not suffer us to rest.

In this desolate spot I discovered one object of interest in a singular little bird, of slender form and pale yellowish-brown colour. Perched on a stem above the grass it gave utterance at regular intervals to a clear, long, plaintive whistle, audible nearly a quarter of a mile away; and this one unmodulated note was its only song or call. When any attempt to approach it was made it would drop down into the grass, and conceal itself with a shyness very unusual in a desert place where small birds have never been persecuted by man. It might have been a wren, or tree-creeper, or reed-finch, or pipit; I could not tell, so jealously did it hide all its pretty secrets from me.

The sight of a group of sand-hills, some two or three miles to our right, tempted us to turn aside from the narrow path we had followed for upwards of six hours: from the summit of these hills we hoped to be able to discover the end of our journey. On approaching the group we found that it formed part of a range stretching south and north as far as the eye could see. Concluding that we were now close to the sea once more, we agreed that our best plan would be, after taking a refreshing bath, to follow the beach on to the mouth of the Rio Negro, where there was a pilot's house. An hour's walk brought us to the hill. Climbing to the top, what was our dismay at beholding not the open blue Atlantic we had so confidently expected to see, but an ocean of barren yellow sand-hills, extending away before us to where earth and heaven mingled in azure mist! I, however, had no right to repine now, as I had set out that morning desirous only of drinking from that wild cup, which is both bitter and sweet to the taste. But I was certainly the greatest sufferer that day, as I had insisted on taking my large cloth poncho, and it proved a great burden to carry; then my feet had become so swollen and painful, through wearing heavy riding boots, that was at last compelled to pull off these impediments, and to travel barefooted on the hot sand and gravel.

Turning our backs on the hills, we started, wearily enough, to seek the trail we had abandoned, directing our course so as to strike it three or four miles in advance of the point where we had turned aside. Escaping from the long grass we again found gravelly, undulating plains, with scattered dark-leafed bushes, and troops of little singing and trilling birds. Armadillos were also seen, but now they scuttled across our path with impunity, for we had no inclination to chase them. It was near sunset when we struck the path again; but although we had now been over twelve hours walking in the heat, without tasting food or water, we still struggled on. Only when it grew dark, and a sudden cold wind sprang up from the sea, making us feel stiff and sore, did we finally come to a halt. Wood was abundant, and we made a large fire, and the Italian roasted the two armadillos he had patiently been carrying all day. They smelt very tempting when done; but I feared that the fat luscious meat would only increase the torturing thirst I suffered, and so while the others picked the bones I solaced myself with a pipe, sitting in pensive silence by the fire. Supper done, we stretched ourselves out by the fire, with nothing but my large poncho over us, and despite the hardness of our bed and the cold wind blowing over us, we succeeded in getting some refreshing sleep.

At three o'clock in the morning we were up and on our way again, drowsy and footsore, but fortunately feeling less thirsty than on the previous day. When we had been walking half an hour there was a welcome indication of the approach of day—not in the sky, where the stars were still sparkling with midnight brilliancy, but far in advance of us a little bird broke out into a song marvellously sweet and clear. The song was repeated, at short intervals, and by-and-by it was taken up by

CHAÑAR TREES

other voices, until from every bush came such soft delicious strains that I was glad of all I had gone through in my long walk, since it had enabled me to hear this exquisite melody of the desert. This early morning singer is a charming grey and white finch, the *Diuca minor*, very common in Patagonia, and the finest voiced of all the fringilline birds found there; and that is saying a great deal. The *Diucas* were sure prophets: before long the first pale streaks of light appeared in the east, but when the light grew we looked in vain for the long-wished river. The sun rose on the same great undulating plain, with its scattered sombre bushes and carpet of sere grass—that ragged carpet showing beneath it the barren sand and gravelly soil from which it draws its scanty subsistence.

For upwards of six hours we trudged doggedly on over this desert plain, suffering much from thirst and fatigue, but not daring to give ourselves rest. At length the aspect of the country began to change: we were approaching the river settlement. The scanty grass grew scantier, and the scrubby bushes looked as if they had been browsed on; our narrow path was also crossed at all angles by cattle tracts, and grew fainter as we proceeded, and finally disappeared altogether. A herd of cattle, slowly winding their way in long trains towards the open country, was then seen. Here, too, a pretty little tree called chañar (*Gurliaca decorticans*), began to get common, growing singly or in small groups. It was about ten to sixteen feet high, very graceful, with smooth, polished green bole, and pale grey-green mimosa foliage. It bears a golden fruit as big as a cherry, with a peculiar delightful flavour, but it was not yet the season for ripe fruits, and its branches were laden only with the great nests of the industrious woodman. Though it was now the end of December and past the egg season, in my craving for a drop of moisture I began to pull down and demolish the nests—no light task, considering how large and compactly made they were. I was rewarded for my pains by finding three little pearly-white eggs, and, feeling grateful for small mercies, I quickly broke them on my parched tongue.

Half an hour later, about eleven o'clock, as we slowly dragged on, a mounted man appeared driving a small troop of horses towards the river. We hailed him, and he rode up to us, and informed us that we were only about a mile from the river, and after hearing our story he proceeded to catch horses for us to ride. Springing on to their bare backs we followed him at a swinging gallop over that last happy mile of our long journey.

We came very suddenly to the end, for on emerging from the thickets of dwarf thorn trees through which we had ridden in single file the magnificent Rio Negro lay before us. Never river seemed fairer to look upon: broader than the Thames at Westminster, and extending away on either hand until it melted and was lost in the blue horizon, its low shores clothed in all the glory of groves and fruit orchards and vineyards and fields of ripening maize. Far out in the middle of the swift blue current floated flocks of black-necked swans, their white plumage shining like foam in the sunlight; while just beneath us, scarcely a stone's throw off, stood the thatched farmhouse of our conductor, the smoke curling up peacefully from the kitchen chimney. A grove of large old cherry trees, in which the house was embowered, added to the charm of the picture; and as we rode down to the gate we noticed the fully ripe cherries glowing like live coals amid the deep green foliage.

II

HOW I BECAME AN IDLER

IF things had gone well with me, if I had spent my twelve months on the Rio Negro, as I had meant to do, watching and listening to the birds of that district, these desultory chapters, which might be described as a record of what I did not do, would never have been written. For I should have been wholly occupied with my special task, moving in a groove too full of delights to allow of its being left, even for an occasional run and taste of liberty; and seeing one class of objects too well would have made all others look distant, obscure, and of little interest. But it was not to be as I had planned it. An accident, to be described by-and-by, disabled me for a period, and the winged people could no longer be followed with secret steps to their haunts, and their actions watched through a leafy screen. Lying helpless on my back through the long sultry midsummer days, with the white-washed walls of my room for landscape and horizon, and a score or two of buzzing house-flies, perpetually engaged in their intricate airy dance, for only company, I was forced to think on a great variety of subjects, and to occupy my mind with other problems than that of migration. These other problems, too, were in many ways like the flies that shared my apartment, and yet always remained strangers to me, as I to them, since between their minds and mine a great gulf was fixed. Small unpainful riddles of the earth; flitting, sylph-like things, that began life as abstractions, and developed, like imago from maggot, into entities: I always flitting among them, as they performed their mazy dance, whirling in circles, falling and rising, poised motionless, then suddenly cannoning against me for an instant, mocking my power to grasp them, and darting off again at a tangent. Baffled I would drop out of the game, like a tired fly that goes back to his perch, but like the resting, restive fly I would soon turn towards them again; perhaps to see them all wheeling in a closer order, describing new fantastic figures, with swifter motions, their forms turned to thin black lines, crossing and recrossing in every direction, as if they had all combined to write a series of strange characters in the air, all forming a strange sentence—the secret of secrets! Happily for the progress of knowledge only a very few of these fascinating elusive insects of the brain can appear before us at the same time: as a rule we fix our attention on a single individual, like a falcon amid a flight of pigeons or a countless army of small field finches; or a dragon-fly in the thick of a cloud of mosquitoes, or infinitesimal sand-flies. Hawk and dragon-fly would starve if they tried to capture, or even regarded, more than one at a time.

I caught nothing, and found out nothing; nevertheless, these days of enforced idleness were not unhappy. And after leaving my room, hobbling round with the aid of a stout stick, and sitting in houses, I consorted with men and women, and listened day by day to the story of their small un-avian affairs, until it began to interest me. But not too keenly. I could always quit them without regret to lie on the green sward, to gaze up into the trees or the blue sky, and speculate on all imaginable things. The result was that when no longer any excuse for inaction existed, use had bred a habit in me—the habit of indolence, which was quite common among the people of Patagonia, and appeared to suit the genial climate; and this habit and temper of mind I retained, with occasional slight relapses, during the whole period of my stay.

Our waking life is sometimes like a dream, which proceeds logically enough until the stimulus of some new sensation, from without or within, throws it into temporary confusion, or suspends its action; after which it goes on again, but with fresh characters, passions, and motives, and a changed argument.

After feasting on cherries, and resting at the estancia, or farm, where we first touched the shore, we went on to the small town of El Carmen, which has existed since the last century, and is built on the side of a hill, or bluff, facing the river. On the opposite shore, where there is no cliff nor high bank, and the low level green valley extends back four or five miles to the grey barren uplands, there is another small town called La Merced. In these two settlements I spent about a fortnight, and then, in company with a young Englishman, who had been one or two years in the colony, I started for an eighty miles' ride up the river. Half-way to our destination we put up at a small log hut, which my companion had himself built a year before; but finding, too late, that the ground would produce nothing, he had lately abandoned it, leaving his tools and other belongings locked up in the place.

A curious home and repository was this same little rude cabin. The interior was just roomy enough to enable a man of my height (six feet) to stand upright and swing a cat in without knocking out its brains against the upright rough-barked willow-posts that made the walls. Yet within this limited space was gathered a store of weapons, tackle, and tools, sufficient to have enabled a small colony of men to fight the wilderness and found a city of the future. My friend had an ingenious mind and an amateur's knowledge of a variety of handicrafts. The way to make him happy was to tell him that you had injured something made of iron or brass—a gun-lock, watch, or anything complicated. His eyes would shine, he would rub his hands and be all eagerness to get at the new patient to try his surgical skill on him. Now he had to give two or three days to all these wood and metal friends of his, to give a fresh edge to his chisels, and play the dentist to his saws; to spread them all out and count and stroke them lovingly, as a breeder pats his beasties, and feed and anoint them with oil to make them shine and look glad. This was preliminary to the packing for transportation, which was also a rather slow process.

Leaving my friend at his delightful task I rambled about the neighbourhood taking stock of the birds. It was a dreary and desolate spot, with a few old gaunt and half-dead red willows for only trees. The reeds and rushes standing in the black stagnant pools were yellow and dead; and dead also were the tussocks of coarse tow-coloured grass, while the soil beneath was white as ashes and cracked everywhere with the hot suns and long drought. Only the river close by was always cool and green and beautiful.

At length, one hot afternoon, we were sitting on our rugs on the clay floor of the hut, talking of our journey on the morrow, and of the better fare and other delights we should find at the end of the day at the house of an English settler we were going to visit. While talking I took up his revolver to examine it for the first time, and he had just begun to tell me that it was a revolver with a peculiar character of its own, and with idiosyncrasies, one of which was that the slightest touch, or even vibration of the air, would cause it to go off when on the cock—he was just telling me this, when off it went with a terrible bang and sent a conical bullet into my left knee, an inch or so beneath the knee-cap. The pain was not much, the sensation resembling that caused by a smart blow on the knee; but on attempting to get up I fell back. I could not stand. Then the blood began to flow in a thin but continuous stream from the round symmetrical bore which seemed to go straight into the bone of the joint, and nothing that we could do would serve to stop it. Here we were in a pretty fix! Thirty six miles from the settlement, and with no conveyance that my friend could think of except a cart at a house several miles up the river, but on the wrong side! He, however, in his anxiety to do something, imagined, or hoped, that by some means the cart might be got over the river, and so, after thoughtfully putting a can of water by my side, he left me lying on my saddle-rugs, and, after fastening the door on the outside to prevent the intrusion of unwelcome prowlers, he mounted his horse and rode away. He had promised that, with or without some wheeled thing, he would be back not long after dark. But he did not return all night; he had found a boat and boatman to transport him to the other side only to learn that his plan was impracticable, and then returning with the disappointing tidings, found no boat to recross, and so in the end was obliged to tie his horse to a bush and lie down to wait for morning.

For me night came only too soon. I had no candle, and the closed, windowless cabin was intensely dark. My wounded leg had become inflamed and pained a great deal, but the bleeding continued until the handkerchiefs we had bound round it were saturated. I was fully dressed, and as the night grew chilly I pulled my big cloth poncho, that had a soft fluffy lining, over me for warmth. I soon gave up expecting my friend, and knew that there would be no relief until morning. But I could neither doze nor think, and could only listen. From my experience during those black anxious hours I can imagine how much the sense of hearing must be to the blind and to animals that exist in dark caves. At length, about midnight, I was startled by a slight curious sound in the intense silence and darkness. It was in the cabin and close to me. I thought at first it was like the sound made by a rope drawn slowly over the clay floor. I lighted a wax match, but the sound had ceased, and I saw nothing. After awhile I heard it again, but it now seemed to be out of doors and going round the hut, and I paid little attention to it. It soon ceased, and I heard it no more. So silent and dark was it thereafter that the hut I reposed in might have been a roomy coffin in which I had been buried a hundred feet beneath the surface of the earth. Yet I was no longer alone, if I had only known it, but had now a messmate and bedfellow who had subtly crept in to share the warm of the cloak and of my person—one with a broad arrow-shaped head, set with round lidless eyes like polished yellow pebbles, and a long smooth limbless body, strangely segmented and vaguely written all over with mystic characters in some dusky tint on an indeterminate greyish-tawny ground.

At length, about half-past three to four o'clock, a most welcome sound was heard—the familiar twittering of a pair of scissor-tail tyrant birds from a neighbouring willow-tree; and after an interval, the dreamy, softly rising and falling, throaty warblings of the white-rumped swallow. A loved and beautiful bird is this, that utters his early song circling round and round in the dusky air, when the stars begin to pale; and his song, perhaps, seems sweeter than all others, because it corresponds in time to that rise in the temperature and swifter flow of the blood—the inward resurrection experienced on each morning of our individual life. Next in order the red-billed finches begin to sing—a curious, gobbling, impetuous performance, more like a cry than a song. These are pretty reed birds, olive-green, buff-breasted, with long tails and bright red beaks. The intervals between their spasmodic bursts of sound were filled up with the fine frail melody of the small brown and grey crested song-sparrows. Last of all was heard the long, leisurely-uttered chanting cry of the brown carrion-hawk, as he flew past, and I knew that the morning was beautiful in the east. Little by little the light began to appear through the crevices, faint at first, like faintly-traced pallid lines on a black ground, then brighter and broader until I, too, had a dim twilight in the cabin.

Not until the sun was an hour up did my friend return to me to find me hopeful still, and with all my faculties about me, but unable to move without

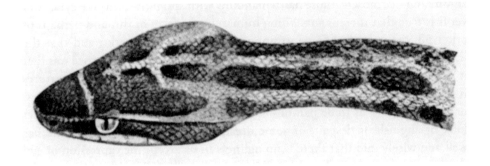

SERPENT WITH A CROSS

assistance. Putting his arms around me he helped me up, and just as I had got erect on my sound leg, leaning heavily on him, out from beneath the poncho lying at my feet glided a large serpent of a venomous kind, the *Craspedocephalus alternatus*, called in the vernacular the *serpent with a cross*. Had my friend's arms not been occupied with sustaining me he, no doubt, would have attacked it with the first weapon that offered, and in all probability killed it, with the result that I should have suffered from a kind of vicarious remorse ever after. Fortunately it was not long in drawing its coils out of sight and danger into a hole in the wall. My hospitality had been unconscious nor, until that moment, had I known that something had touched me, and that virtue had gone out from me; but I rejoice to think that the secret deadly creature, after lying all night with me, warming its chilly blood with my warmth, went back unbruised to its den.

Speaking of this serpent with a strange name, I recall the fact that Darwin made its acquaintance during his Patagonian rambles about sixty years ago; and in describing its fierce and hideous aspect, remarks, "I do not think I ever saw anything more ugly, excepting, perhaps, some of the vampire bats." He speaks of the great breadth of the jaws at the base, the triangular snout, and the linear pupil in the midst of the mottled coppery iris, and suggests that its ugly and horrible appearance is due to the resemblance of its face, in its shape, to the human countenance.

This idea of the ugliness or repulsiveness of an inferior animal, due to its resemblance to man in face, is not, I believe, uncommon; and I suppose that the reason that would be given for the feeling is that an animal of that kin looks like a vile copy of ourselves, or like a parody maliciously designed to mock us. It is an erroneous idea, or, at all events, is only a half-truth, as we recognize at once when we look at animals that are more or less human-like in countenance, and yet cause no repulsion. Seals may be mentioned—the mermaids and mermen of the old mariners; also the sloth with its round simple face, to which its human shape imparts a somewhat comical and pathetic look. Many monkeys seem ugly to us, but we think the lemurs beautiful, and greatly admire the marmosets, those hairy manikins with sprightly, bird-like eyes. And yet it is true that there is something human in the faces of this and perhaps of other pit-vipers, and of some vampire bats, as Darwin remarks; and that the horror they excite in us is due to this resemblance; what he failed to see was that it is the expression rather than the shape that horrifies. For in these creatures it simulates such expressions as excite fear and abhorrence in our own species, or pity so intense as to be painful—ferocity, stealthy, watchful malignity, a set look of anguish or despair, or some dreadful form of insanity. Someone has well and wisely said that there is no ugliness in us except the expression of evil thoughts and passions; for these do most assuredly write themselves on the countenance. Looking at a serpent of this kind, and I have looked at many a one, the fancy is born in me that I am regarding what was once a fellow-being, perhaps one of those cruel desperate wretches I have encountered on the outskirts of civilization, who for his crimes has been changed into the serpent form, and cursed with immortality.

As a rule the deceptive resemblances and self plagiarisms of nature, when we light by chance on them, give us only pleasure, heightened by wonder or a sense of mystery; but the case of this serpent forms an exception: in spite of the tenderness I cherish towards the entire ophidian race, the sensation is not agreeable.

To return. My friend made a fire to boil water, and after we had had some breakfast, he galloped off once more in a new direction; he had at last remembered that on our side of the river there lived a settler who owned a bullock-cart, and to him he went. About ten o'clock he returned, and was shortly followed by the man with his lumbering cart drawn by a couple of bullocks. In this conveyance, suffering much from the heat and dust and joltings on the rough hard road, I was carried back to the settlement. Oxen travel slowly, and we were on the road all day and all night, and only reached our destination when the eastern sky had begun to grow bright, and the swallows from a thousand roosting-places were rising in wide circles into the still, dusky air, making it vocal with their warblings.

My miserable journey ended at the Mission House of the South American Missionary Society, in the village on the south bank of the river, facing the old town; and the change from the jolting cart to a comfortable bed was an unspeakable relief, and soon induced refreshing sleep. Later in the day, on awakening, I found myself in the hands of a gentleman who was a skilful surgeon as well as a divine one, who had extracted more bullets and mended broken bones than most surgeons who do not practise on battle-fields. My bullet, however, refused to be extracted, or even found in its hiding-place, and every morning for a fortnight I had a bad quarter of an hour, when my host would present himself in my room with a quiet smile on his lips and holding in his hands a bundle of probes—oh, those probes!—of all forms, sizes, and materials—wood, ivory, steel, and gutta-percha. These painful moments over, with no result except the re-opening of a wound that wished to heal, there would be nothing more for me to do but to lie watching the flies, as I have said, and dreaming.

To conclude this vari-coloured chapter, I may here remark that some of the happiest moments of my life have been occasioned by those very circumstances which one would imagine would have made me most unhappy—by grave accidents, and sickness, which have disabled and cast me a burden upon strangers; and by adversity—

> Which, like a toad, ugly and venomous,
> Yet wears a precious jewel in its head.

Familiar words, but here newly interpreted; for this jewel which I have found—man's love for man, and the law of helpful kindness written in the hearts—is worthy to be prized above all our possessions, and is most beautiful, outshining the lapidary's gems, and of so sovereign a virtue that cynicism itself grows mute and ashamed in its light.

III

VALLEY OF THE BLACK RIVER

STILL a lingerer in the hospitable shade of the Mission House, my chief pleasure during the early days of February was in observing the autumnal muster of the purple swallows—*Progne furcata*—a species which was abundant at this point, breeding in the cliffs overhanging the river; also, like so many other swallows in all places, under the eaves of houses. It is a large, beautiful bird, its whole upper plumage of a rich, glossy, deep purple hue, its under surface black. No such large swallows as this, with other members of its genus, are known in the Old World; and a visitor from Europe would probably, on first seeing one of these birds, mistake it for a swift; but it has not got the narrow, scythe-shaped wings of the swift, nor does it rush through the air in the swift's mad way; on the contrary, its flight is much calmer, with fewer quick doublings than that of other swallows. It also differs from most members of its family in possessing a set song of several modulated notes, which are occasionally warbled in a leisurely manner as the bird soars high in the air: as a melodist it should rank high among the hirundines.

The trees of the Mission House proved very attractive to these birds; the tall Lombardy poplars were specially favoured, which seems strange, for in a high wind (and it was very windy just then) the slim unresting tree forms as bad a perching-place as a bird could well settle on. Nevertheless, to the poplars they would come when the wind was most violent; first hovering or wheeling about in an immense flock, then, as occasion offered, dropping down, a few at a time, to cling, like roosting locusts, to the thin vertical branches, clustering thicker and thicker until the high trees looked black with them; then a mightier gust would smite and sway the tall tops down, and the swallows, blown from their insecure perch, would rise in a purple cloud to scatter chattering all over the windy heavens, only to return and congratulate, hovering and clinging as before.

Lying on the grass, close to the river bank, I would watch them by the hour, noting their unrest and indecision, the strangeness and wild spirit that made the wind and vexed poplars congenial to them; for something new and strange had come to trouble them—the subtle breath

> That in a powerful language, felt, not heard,
> Instructs the fowls of heaven.

But as to the character of that breath I vainly questioned Nature—she being the only woman who can keep a secret, even from a lover.

Rain came at last, and fell continuously during an entire night. Next morning (February 14th) when I went out and looked up at the sky, covered with grey hurrying clouds, I saw a flock of forty or fifty large swallows speeding north; and after these I saw no more; for on that first wet morning, before I had risen, the purple cloud had forsaken the valley.

I missed them greatly, and wished that they had delayed their going, since it was easier and more hopeful to ponder on the mystery of their instinct when they were with me. That break in the tenor of their lives; the enforced change of habits; the conflict between two opposite emotions—the ties of place that held them back, seen and guessed in their actions, and the voice that called them away,

SWALLOWS CONGREGATING

speaking ever more imperatively, which so wrought in them that at moments they were beside themselves—noting all this, hearing and seeing it at all hours of the day, I seemed to be nearer to the discovery of some hidden truth than when they were no longer in sight. But now they were gone, and with their departure had vanished my last excuse for resting longer inactive—at that spot, at all events.

I started afresh on my up-river journey, and paid a long visit to an English estancia about sixty miles from the town. I spent much of my time there in solitary rambles, tasting once more of the "sweet and bitter cup of wild Nature." Her colour was grey, her mood pensive as winter deepened, and there was nothing in the cup to inflame the fancy. But it was tonic. My rides were often to the hills, or terraced uplands, outside of the level valley; but my description of that grey desolate solitude and its effects on me must be reserved for a later chapter, when I shall have dropped once for all this thread of narrative, slight and loosely held as it is. In the present chapter and the succeeding one I shall treat of the aspects of nature in the valley itself. For I did not remain too long at any one point, but during the autumn, winter, and spring months I resided at various points, and visited the mouth of the river and adjacent plains on both sides, then went up river again to a distance of something over a hundred miles.

The valley, in this space, does not vary much in appearance; it may be described as the level bed of an ancient river, five or six miles wide, cut out in the plateau, with the existing river—a swift, deep stream, two hundred to three hundred yards broad—serpentining along its middle. But it does not keep to the middle; in its windings it approaches now the north, now the south, plateau, and at some points touches the extreme limits of the valley, and even cuts into the bank-like front of the high land, which forms a sheer cliff above the current, in some spots a hundred feet high.

The river was certainly miscalled Cusar-leofú or Black River, by the aborigines, unless the epithet referred only to its swiftness and dangerous character; for it is not black at all in appearance, like its Amazonian namesake. The water, which flows from the Andes across a continent of stone and gravel, is wonderfully pure, in colour a clear sea-green. So green does it look to the eye in some lights that when dipped up in a glass vessel one marvels to see it changed, no longer green, but crystal as dew- or rain-drop. Doubtless man is naturally scientific, and finds out why things are not what they seem, and gets to the bottom of all mysteries; but his older, deeper, primitive, still persistent nature is non-scientific and mythical, and, in spite of reason, he wonders at the change;—it is a miracle, a manifestation of the intelligent life and power that is in all things.

The river has its turbid days, although few and far between. One morning, on going down to the water, I was astonished to find it no longer the lovely hue of the previous evening, but dull red—red with the red earth that some swollen tributary hundreds of miles to the west had poured into its current. This change lasts only a day or two, after which the river runs green and pure again.

The valley at the end of a long hot windy summer had an excessively dry and barren appearance. The country, I was told, had suffered from scarcity of rain for three years: at some points even the roots of the dry dead grass had been blown away, and when the wind was strong a cloud of yellow dust hung all day over the valley. In such places sheep were dying of starvation: cattle and horses fared better, as they went out into the uplands to browse on the bushes. The valley soil is thin, being principally sand and gravel, with a slight admixture of vegetable mould; and its original vegetation was made up of coarse perennial grasses, herbaceous shrubs and rushes: the domestic cattle introduced by the white settlers destroyed these slow-growing grasses and plants, and, as has happened in most temperate regions of the globe colonized by Europeans, the sweet, quick-growing, short-lived grasses and clovers of the Old World sprang up and occupied the soil. Here, however, owing to its poverty, the excessive dryness of the climate, and the violence of the winds that prevail in summer, the new imported vegetation has proved but a sorry substitute for the old and vanished. It does not grow large enough to retain the scanty moisture, it is too short-lived, and the frail quickly-perishing rootlets do not bind the earth together, like the tough fibrous blanket formed by the old grasses. The heat burns it to dust and ashes, the wind blows it away, blade and root, and the surface soil with it, in many places disclosing the yellow underlying sand with all that was buried in it of old. For the results of this stripping of the surface has been that the sites of numberless villages of the former inhabitants of the valley have been brought to light. I have visited a dozen such village sites in the course of one hour's walk, so numerous were they. Where the village had been a populous one, or inhabited for a long period, the ground was a perfect bed of chipped stones, and among these fragments were found arrow-heads, flint, knives and scrapers, mortars and pestles, large round stones with a groove in the middle, pieces of hard polished stone used as anvils, perforated shells, fragments of pottery, and bones of animals. My host remarked one day that the valley that year had produced nothing but a plentiful crop of arrow-heads. The anthropologist could not have wished for a more favourable year or for a better crop. I collected a large number of these objects; and some three or four hundred arrow-heads which I picked up are at present, I believe, in the famous Pitt-Rivers collection. But I was over-careful. The finest of my treasures, the most curious and beautiful objects I could select, packed apart for greater safety, were unfortunately lost in transit—a severe blow, which hurt me more than the wound I had received on the knee.

At some of the villages I examined, within a few yards of the ground where the huts had stood, I found deposits of bones of animals that had been used as food. These were of the rhea, huanaco, deer, peccary, *Dolichotis* or Patagonian hare, armadillo, coypú, vizcacha, with others of smaller mammals and birds. Most numerous among them were the bones of the small cavy (*Cavia australis*), a form of the guinea-pig; and of the tuco-tuco (*Ctenomys magellanica*), a small rodent with the habits of the mole.

A most interesting fact was that the arrow heads I picked up in different villages were of two widely different kinds—the large and rudely fashioned, resembling the Paleolithic arrow-heads of Europe, and the highly-finished, or Neolithic, arrow-heads of various forms and sizes, but in most specimens an inch and a half to two inches long. Here there were the remains of the two great periods of the Stone Age, the last of which continued down till the discovery and colonization of the country by Europeans. The weapons and other objects of the latter period were the most abundant, and occurred in the valley: the ruder more ancient weapons were found on the hill-sides, in places where the river cuts into the plateau. The site where I picked up the largest number had been buried to a depth of seven or eight feet; only where the water after heavy rains had washed great masses of sand and gravel away, the arrow heads, with other weapons and implements, had been exposed. These deeply-buried settlements were doubtless very ancient.

Coming back to the more modern work, I was delighted to find traces of a something like division of labour in different villages; of the individuality of the worker, and a distinct artistic or æsthetic taste. I was led to this conclusion by the discovery of a village site where no large round stones, knives and scrapers were found, and no large arrow-heads of the usual type. The only arrow heads at this spot were about half an inch long, and were probably used only to shoot small birds and mammals. Not only were they minute but most exquisitely finished, with a fine serration, and, without an exception, made of some beautiful stone—crystal, agate, and green, yellow, and horn-coloured flint. It was impossible to take half-a-dozen of these gems of colour and workmanship in the hand and not be impressed at once with the idea that beauty had been as much an aim to the worker as utility. Along with these fine arrow-heads I found nothing except one small well-pointed dagger of red stone, its handle a cross, about four inches long, and as slender and almost as well-rounded as an ordinary lead pencil.

When on this quest I sometimes attempted to picture to myself something of the outer and inner life of the long-vanished inhabitants. The red men of to-day may be of the same race and blood, the lineal descendants of the workers in stone in Patagonia; but they are without doubt so changed, and have lost so much, that their progenitors would not know them, nor acknowledge them as relations. Here, as in North America, contact with a superior race has debased them and ensured their destruction. Some of their wild blood will continue to flow in the veins of those who have taken their place; but as a race they will be blotted out from earth, as utterly extinct in a few decades as the mound-makers of the Mississippi valley, and the races that built the forest-grown cities of Yucutan and Central America. The men of the past in the Patagonian valley were alone with nature, makers of their own weapons and self-sustaining, untouched by any outside influence, and with no knowledge of any world beyond their valley and

AN INDIAN BURIAL-PLACE

the adjacent uninhabited uplands. And yet, judging even from that dim partial glimpse I had had of their vanished life, in the weapons and fragments I had picked up, it seemed evident that the mind was not wholly dormant in them, and that they were slowly progressing to a higher condition.

Beyond that fact I could not go: all efforts to know more, or to imagine more, ended in failure, as all such efforts must end. On another occasion, as I propose to show in a later chapter, the wished vision of the past came unsought and unexpectedly to me, and for a while I saw nature as the savage sees it, and as he saw it in that stone age I pondered over, only without the supernaturalism that has so large a place in his mind. By taking thought I am convinced that we can make no progress in this direction simply because we cannot voluntarily escape from our own personality, our environment, our outlook on Nature.

Not only were my efforts idle, but merely to think on the subject sometimes had the effect of bringing a shadow, a something of melancholy, over my mind, the temper which is fatal to investigation, causing "all things to droop and languish." In such a mood I would make my way to one of the half-a-dozen ancient burial-places existing in the neighbourhood of the house I was staying at. As a preference

I would go to the largest and most populous, where half an acre of earth was strewn thick with crumbling skeletons. Here by searching closely a few arrowheads and ornaments that had been interred with the dead, could also be found. And here I would sit and walk about on the hot barren yellow sand—the faithless sand to which the bitter secret had so long ago been vainly entrusted; careful in walking not to touch an exposed skull with my foot, although the hoof of the next wild thing that passed would shatter it to pieces like a vessel of fragile glass. The polished intensely white surfaces of such skulls as had been longest exposed to the sun reflected the noonday light so powerfully that it almost pained the eyes to look at them. In places where they were thickly crowded together, I would stop to take them up and examine them, one by one, only to put them carefully down again; and sometimes holding one in my hand, I would pour out the yellow sand that filled its cavity; and watching the shining stream as it fell, only the vainest of vain thoughts and conjectures were mine.

IV

ASPECTS OF THE VALLEY

TO go back for a brief space to those Golgothas that I frequently visited in the valley, not as collector nor archæologist, and in no scientific spirit, but only, as it seemed, to indulge in mournful thoughts. If by looking into the empty cavity of one of those broken unburied skulls I had been able to see, as in a magic glass, an image of the world as it once existed in the living brain, what should I have seen? Such a question would not and could not, I imagine, be suggested by the sight of a bleached broken human skull in any other region; but in Patagonia it does not seem grotesque, nor merely idle, nor quite fanciful, like Buffon's notion of a geometric figure impressed on the hive-bee's brain. On the contrary, it strikes one there as natural; and the answer to it is easy, and only one answer is possible.

In the cavity, extending from side to side, there would have appeared a band of colour; its margins grey, growing fainter and bluer outwardly, and finally fading into nothing; between the grey edges the band would be green; and along this green middle band, not always keeping to the centre, there would appear a sinuous shiny line, like a serpent with glittering skin lying at rest on the grass. For the river must have been to the aboriginal inhabitants of the valley the one great central unforgettable fact in nature and man's life. If as nomads or colonists from some cis- or trans-Andean country they had originally brought hither traditions, and some supernatural system that took its form and colour from a different nature, these had been modified, if not wholly dissolved and washed away in that swift eternal green current, by the side of which they continued to dwell from generation to generation, forgetting all ancient things. The shining stream was always in sight, and when, turning their backs on it, they climbed out of the valley, they saw only grey desolation—a desert where life was impossible to man—fading into the blue haze of the horizon; and there was nothing beyond it. On that grey strip, on the borders of the unknown beyond, they could search for tortoises, and hunt a few wild animals, and gather a few wild fruits, and hard woods and spines for weapons; and then return to the river, as children go back to their mother. All things were reflected in its waters, the infinite blue sky, the clouds and heavenly bodies; the trees and tall herbage on its banks, and their dark faces; and just as they were mirrored in it, so its current was mirrored in their minds. The old man, grown blind with age, from constantly seeing its image so bright and persistent, would be unconscious of his blindness. It was thus more to him than all other objects and forces in nature; the Inca might worship sun and lightning and rainbow; to the inhabitant of the valley the river was more than these, the most powerful thing in nature, the most beneficent, and his chief god.

I do not know, nor can any one know, whether the former dwellers in the valley left any descendants, any survivors of that age that left some traces of a brightening intellect on its stone work. Probably not; the few Indians now inhabiting the valley are most probably modern colonists of another family or nation; yet it did not surprise me to hear that some of these half-tame, half-christianized savages had, not long before my visit, sacrificed a white bull to the river, slaying it on the bank and casting its warm, bleeding body into the current.

Even the European colonists have not been unaffected psychologically by the peculiar conditions they live in, and by the river, on which they are dependent. When first I became cognizant of this feeling, which was very soon, I was disposed to laugh a little at the very large place *the river* occupied in all men's minds; but after a few months of life on its banks it was hardly less to me than to others, and I experienced a kind of shame when I recalled my former want of reverence, as if I had made a jest of something sacred. Nor to this day can I think of the Patagonian river merely as one of the rivers I know. Other streams, by comparison, seem vulgar, with no higher purpose than to water man and beast, and to serve, like canals, as a means of transport.

One day, to the house where I was staying near the town, there came a native lady on a visit, bringing with her six bright blue-eyed children. As we, the elders, sat in the living-room, sipping maté and talking, one of the youngsters, an intelligent-looking boy of nine, came in from play, and getting him by me I amused him for a while with some yarns and with talk about beasts and birds. He asked me where I lived. My home, I said, was in the Buenos Ayrean pampas, far north of Patagonia.

"Is it near the river," he asked, "right on the bank, like this house?"

I explained that it was on a great, grassy, level plain, that there was no river there, and that when I went out on horseback I did not have to ride up and down a valley, but galloped away in any direction—north, south, east, or west. He listened with a twinkle in his eyes, then with a merry laugh ran out again to join the others at their game. It was as if I had told him that I lived up in a tree that grew to the clouds, or under the sea, or some such impossible thing; it was nothing but a joke to him. His mother, sitting near, had been listening to us, and when the boy laughed and ran out, I remarked to her that to a child born and living always in that valley, shut in by the thorny, waterless uplands, it was, perhaps, inconceivable that in other places people could exist out of a valley and away from a river. She looked at me with a puzzled expression in her eyes, as if trying to see something mentally which her eyes had never seen—trying, in fact, to create something out of nothing. She agreed with me in some hesitating words, and I felt that I had put my foot in it; for only then I recalled the fact that she also had been born in the valley—the great-grand-daughter of one of the original founders of the colony—and was probably as incapable as the child of imagining any other conditions than those she had always been accustomed to.

It struck me that the children here have a very healthy, happy life, especially those whose homes are in the narrow parts of the valley, who are able to ramble every day into the thorny uplands in search of birds' eggs and other pretty things, and the wild flavours and little adventures that count for so much with the very young. In birds' eggs, the greatest prizes are those of the partridge-like tinamous, the beautifully mottled and crested martineta (*Calodromas elegans*), that lays a dozen eggs as large as those of a fowl, with deep-green polished shells; and the smaller *Nothura darwini*, whose eggs vary in tint from wine-purple to a reddish-purple or liver colour. In summer and autumn fruits and sweet gums are not scarce. One grey-leafed herbaceous shrub is much sought after for its sap, that oozes from the stem and hardens in small globes and lumps that look and taste like white sugar. There is a small disc-shaped cactus, growing close to the surface, and well defended with sharp spines, which bears a pinkish-yellow fruit with a pleasant taste. There is also a large cactus, four or five feet high, so dark-green as to appear almost black among the pale-grey bushes. It bears a splendid crimson flower, and a crimson fruit that is insipid and not considered worth eating; but being of so beautiful a colour to see it is sufficient pleasure. The plant is not very common, and one does not see too many of the fruits even in a long day's ramble:

Like stones of worth, they thinly placed are.

The chañar bears a fruit like a cherry in size, and, like a cherry, with a stone inside; it has a white pulp and a golden skin; the flavour is peculiar and delicious, and seemed to be greatly appreciated by the birds, so that the children get little. Another wild fruit is that of the *piquellin* (*Condalia spinosa*), the dark-leafed bush which was mentioned in the first chapter. Its oval-shaped berries are less than currants in size, but are in such profusion that the broad tops of the bushes become masses of deep colour in autumn. There are two varieties, one crimson, the other purple-black, like sloes and blackberries. They have a strong but not unpleasant flavour, and the children are so fond of them that, like the babes in the wood, their little lips are all bestained and red with the beautiful juice.

The magnetism of the river (to go back to that subject) is probably intensified by the prevailing monotonous greys, greens, and browns of nature on either side of it. It has the powerful effect of brightness, which fascinates us, as it does the moth, and the eye is drawn to it as to a path of shining silver—that is, of silver in some conditions of the atmosphere, and of polished steel in others. At ordinary times there is no other brightness in nature to draw the sight away and divide the attention. Only twice in the year, for a brief season in spring and again in autumn, there is anything like large masses of bright colour in the vegetation to delight the eyes. The commonest of the grey-foliaged plants that grow on the high grounds along the borders of the valley is the chañar (*Gurliaca decorticans*), a tree in form, but scarcely more than a bush in size. In late October it bears a profusion of flowers in clusters, in shape, size, and brilliant yellow colour resembling the flower of the broom. At this season the uplands along the valley have a strangely gay appearance. Again, there is yellow in the autumn—the deeper yellow of xanthophyll—when the leaves of the red willows growing on the banks of the river change their colour before falling. This willow (*Salix humboldtiana*) is the only large wild tree in the country; but whether it grew here prior to the advent of the Spanish or not, I do not know. But its existence is now doomed as a large tree of a century's majestic growth, forming a suitable perch and look-out for the harpy and grey eagles, common in the valley, and the still more common vultures and *Polybori*, and of the high-roosting, noble black-faced ibis; a home and house, too, of the Magellanic eagle-owl and the spotted wild cat (*Felis geoffroyi*); and where even the puma could lie at ease on a horizontal branch thirty or forty feet above the earth. Being of soft wood, it can be cut down very easily; and when felled and lashed in rafts on the river, it is floated down stream to supply the inhabitants with a cheap wood for fuel, building, and other purposes.

At the highest point I reached in my rambles along the valley, about a hundred and twenty miles from the coast, there was a very extensive grove or wood of this willow, many of the trees very large, and some dead from age. I visited this spot with an English friend, who resided some twenty miles lower down, and spent a day and a half wading about waist-deep through the tall, coarse grasses and rushes under the leafless gaunt trees, for the season was midwinter. The weather was the worst I had experienced in the country, being piercingly cold, with a violent wind and frequent storms of rain and sleet. The rough, wet boles of the trees rose up tall and straight like black pillars from the rank herbage beneath, and on the higher branches innumerable black vultures (*Cathartes atratus*) were perched, waiting all the dreary day long for fair weather to fly abroad in search of food.

On the ground this vulture does not appear to advantage, especially when bobbing and jumping about, performing the "buzzard lope," when quarrelling with his fellows over a carcase: but when perched aloft, his small naked rugous head and neck and horny curved beak seen well defined above the broad black

BLACK VULTURE

surface of the folded wing, he does not show badly. As I had no wish to make a bag of vultures and saw nothing else, I shot nothing.

A little past noon on the second day we saddled our horses and started on our homeward ride; and although the wind still blew a gale, lashing the river into a long line of foam on the opposite shore, and bringing storms of rain and sleet at intervals, this proved a very delightful ride, one that shines in memory above all other rides I have taken. We went at a swift gallop along the north bank, and never had grey Patagonia looked more soberly and sadly grey than on this afternoon. The soil, except in places where the winter grass had spread over it, had taken a darker brown colour from the rain it had imbibed, and the bosky uplands a deeper grey than ever, while the whole vast sky was stormy and dark. But after a time the westering sun began to shine through the rifts behind us, while before us on the wild flying clouds appeared a rainbow with hues so vivid that we shouted aloud with joy at the sight of such loveliness. For nearly an hour we rode with this vision of glory always before us; grove after grove of leafless black-barked willow-trees on our right hand, and grey thorny hill after hill on our left, did we pass in our swift ride, while great flocks of upland geese continually rose up before us, with shrill whistlings mingled with solemn deep droning cries; and the arch of watery fire still lived, now fading as the flying wrack grew thinner and thinner, then, just when it seemed about to vanish, brightening once more to a new and more wonderful splendour, its arch ever widening to greater proportions as the sun sunk lower in the sky.

I do not suppose that the colours were really more vivid than in numberless other rainbows I have seen; it was, I think, the universal greyness of earth and heaven in that grey winter season, in a region where colour is so sparsely used by Nature, that made it seem so supremely beautiful, so that the sight of it affected us like wine.

The eyes, says Bacon, are ever most pleased with a lively embroidery on a sad and sombre ground. This was taught to us by the green and violet arch on the slaty grey vapour. But Nature is too wise

To blunt the fine point of seldom pleasure.

The day of supernatural splendour and glory comes only after many days that are only natural, and of a neutral colour. It is watched and waited for, and when it comes is like a day of some great festival and rejoicing—the day when peace was made, when our love was returned, when a child was born to us. Such sights are like certain sounds, that not only delight us with their pure and beautiful quality, but wake in us feelings that we cannot fathom nor analyze. They are familiar, yet stranger than the strangest things, with a beauty that is not of the earth, as if a loved friend, long dead, had unexpectedly looked back to us from heaven, transfigured. It strikes me as strange that, so far as we know, the Incas were the only worshippers of the rainbow.

One evening in the autumn of the year, near the town, I was witness of an extraordinary and very magnificent sunset effect. The sky was clear except for a few masses of cloud low down in the west; and these, some time after the sun had disappeared, assumed more vivid and glowing colours, while the pale yellow sky beyond became more luminous and flame-like. All at once, as I stood not far from the bank, looking westward across the river, the water changed from green to an intense crimson hue, this extending on both hands as far as I could see. The tide was running out, and in the middle of the river, where the surface was roughened into waves by the current, it quivered and sparkled like crimson flame, while near the opposite shore, where rows of tall Lombardy poplars threw their shadow on the surface, it was violet-coloured. This appearance lasted for five or six minutes, then the crimson colour grew darker by degrees until it disappeared. I have frequently read and heard of such a phenomenon, and many persons have assured me that they have witnessed it "with their own eyes." But what they have witnessed one does not know. I have often seen the surface of water, of the ocean, or a lake, or river, flushed with a rosy colour at sunset; but to see, some time after sunset, the waters of a river changed to blood and crimson fire, this appearance lasting until the twilight drew on, and the earth and trees looked black by contrast, has been my lot once only on this occasion; and I

THE RIVER BY MOONLIGHT

imagine that if any river on the globe was known to take such an appearance frequently, it would become as celebrated, and draw pilgrims as far to see it; as Chimborazo and the Falls of Niagara.

Between the town and the sea, a distance of about twenty miles, the valley is mostly on the south side of the river; on the north side the current comes very near, and in many places washes the upland. I visited the sea by both ways, and rode for some distance along the coast on both sides of the river. North of the river the beach was shingle and sand, backed by low sand dunes extending away into infinitude; but on the south side, outside the valley, a sheer stupendous precipice faced the ocean. A slight adventure I had with a condor, the only bird of that species I met with in Patagonia, will give some idea of the height of this sheer wall of rock. I was riding with a friend along the cliff when the majestic bird appeared, and swooping downwards hovered at a height of forty feet above our heads. My companion raised his gun and fired, and we heard the shot rattle loudly on the stiff quills of the broad motionless wings. There is no doubt that some of the shot entered its flesh, as it quickly swept down over the edge of the cliff and disappeared from our sight. We got off our horses, and crawling to the edge of the dreadful cliff looked down, but could see nothing of the bird. Remounting we rode on for a little over a mile, until coming to the end of the cliff we went down under it and galloped back over the narrow strip of beach which appears at low tide. Arrived at the spot where the bird had been lost we caught sight of it once more, perched at the mouth of a small cavity in the face of the rocky wall near the summit, and looking at that height no bigger than a buzzard. He was far beyond the reach of shot, and safe, and if not fatally wounded, may soar above that desolate coast, and fight with vultures and grey eagles over the carcases of stranded fishes and seals for half a century to come.

Close to the mouth of the river there is a low flat island, about half a mile in length, covered in most part by a dense growth of coarse grass and rushes. It is inhabited by a herd of swine; and although these animals do not increase, they have been able to maintain their existence for a long period without diminishing in number, in spite of the occasional great tides that flood the whole island, and of multitudes of hungry eagles and caranchos always on the look out for stray sucklings. Many years ago, while some gauchos were driving a troop of half wild cows near the shore on the neighbouring mainland, a heifer took to the water and succeeded in swimming to the island, where she was lost to her owner. About a year later this animal was seen by a man who had gone to the island to cut rushes for thatching purposes. The cow and the pigs, to the number of about twenty-five or twenty-six, were lying fast asleep in a small grassy hollow where he found them, the cow stretched out at full length on the ground, and the pigs grouped or rather heaped round her; for they were all apparently ambitious to rest with their heads pillowed on her, so that she was almost concealed under them. Presently one of the drove, more wakeful than his fellows, became aware of his presence and gave the alarm, whereupon they started up like one animal and vanished into a rush-bed. The cow, thus doomed to live "alone, yet not alone," was subsequently seen on several occasions by the rush-cutters, always with her fierce followers grouped round her like a bodyguard. This continued for some years, and the fame of the cow that had become the leader and queen of the wild island pigs was spread

COW AND PIGS

abroad in the valley; then a human being, who was not a "sentimentalist," betook himself to her little kingdom with a musket loaded with ball, and succeeded in finding and shooting her.

In spite of what we have been taught, it is some times borne in on us that man is a little lower than the brutes.

After hearing this incident one does not at once sit down with a good appetite to roast beef or swine's flesh.

V

A DOG IN EXILE

AT the English estate up the river, where I made so long a stay, there were several dogs, some of them of the common dog of no breed found throughout Argentina, a smooth-haired animal, varying greatly in colour, but oftenest red or black; also differing much in size, but in a majority of cases about as big as a Scotch collie. There were also a few others, dogs of good breeds, and these were especially interesting to me, because they were not restrained nor directed in any way, nor any use made of them in their special lines. Left to their own devices, and to rough it with the others, the result was rather curious. The only one among them that had proved capable of accommodating himself to the new circumstances was a Scotch collie—a fine animal of pure blood.

The common dog of the country is a jack-of-all-trades; a great lover of the chase, but a bad hunter, a splendid scavenger, a good watch-dog and vermin-killer; an indifferent sheep-dog, but invaluable in gathering up and driving cattle. Beyond these things which he picks up, you can really teach him nothing useful, although with considerable trouble you might be able to add a few ornamental subjects, such as giving his paw, and keeping guard over a coat or stick left in his charge. He is a generalized beast, grandson to the jackal, and first cousin to the cur of Europe and the Eastern pariah. To this primitive, or only slightly-improved type of dog, the colley perhaps comes nearest of all the breeds we value; and when he is thrown back on nature he is "all there," and not hindered as the pointer and other varieties are by more deeply-rooted special instincts. At all events, this individual took very kindly to the rude life and work of his new companions, and by means of his hardihood and inexhaustible energy became their leader and superior, especially in hunting. Above anything he loved to chase a fox; and when in the course of a ride in the valley one was started, he invariably threw all the native dogs out and caught and killed it himself. If these dogs had all together taken to a feral life, I do not think the collie would have been worse off than the others.

It was very different with the greyhounds. There were four, all of pure breed; and as they were never taken out to hunt, and could not, like the collie, take their share in the ordinary work of the establishment, they were absolutely useless, and certainly not ornamental. When I first noticed them they were pitiable objects, thin as skeletons, so lame that they could scarcely walk, and wounded and scratched all over with thorns. I was told that they had been out hunting on their own account in the thorny upland, and that this was the result. For three or four days they remained inactive, sleeping the whole time, except when they limped to the kitchen to be fed. But day by day they improved in condition; their scratches healed, their ribbed sides grew smooth and sleek, and they recovered from their lameness; but scarcely had they got well before it was discovered one morning that they had vanished. They had gone off during the night to hunt again on the uplands. They were absent two nights and a day, then returned, looking even more reduced and miserable than when I first saw them, to recover slowly from their hurts and fatigue; and when well again they were off once more; and so it continued during the whole time of my visit. These hounds, if left to themselves, would have soon perished.

Another member of this somewhat heterogeneous canine community was a retriever, one of the handsomest I have ever seen, rather small, and with a most perfect head. The extreme curliness of his coat made him look at a little distance like a dog cut out of a block of ebony, with the surface carved to almost symmetrical knobbiness. Major—that was his name—would have lent himself well to sculpture. He was old, but not too fat, nor inactive; sometimes he would go out with the other dogs, but apparently he could not keep up the pace, as after a few hours he would return always alone, looking rather disconsolate.

I have always been partial to dogs of this breed; not on account of the assistance they have been to me, but because when I have wished to have a dog at my side I have found them more suitable than other kinds for companions. They are not stupid nor restless, but ready to fall in with a quiet mood, and never irritate by a perpetual impatient craving for notice. A fussy, demonstrative dog, that can never efface himself, I object to: he compels your attention, and puts you in a subordinate place: you are his attendant, not he yours.

Major's appearance attracted me from the first, and he, on his side, joyfully responded to my advances, and at once attached himself to me, following me about the place as if he feared to lose sight of me even for a minute. My host, however, hastened to warn me not to take him with me when I went out shooting, as he was old and blind, and subject, moreover, to strange freaks, which made him worse than useless. He had formerly been an excellent retriever, he informed me, but even in his best days not wholly to be trusted, and now he was nothing but bad.

I could scarcely credit the blindness, as he did not show it in his brown intelligent and wistful eyes and always appeared keenly alive and interested in everything going on about him; but by experimenting I found that he could scarcely see further than about six inches from his nose; but his hearing and scent were so good, and guided him so well, that no person on a slight acquaintance would have made the discovery of his defective sight.

Of course, after this, I could have nothing more to do with the retriever, further than patting him on the head, and speaking a kind word to him whenever he chanced to be in my way. But this was not enough for old Major. He was a sporting dog, full of energy, and with undiminished faith in his own powers, in spite of his years, and when a sports man had come to the house, and had deliberately singled him out for friendly notice, he could not and would not believe that it was to go no further. Day after day he clung to the delusion that he was to accompany me in my walks and little shooting excursions in the neighbourhood; and every time I took down a gun he would rush forward from his post by the door with so many demonstrations of joy, and with such imploring looks and gestures, that I found it very hard to rebuke him. It was sad to have him standing there, first cocking up one ear, then the other, striving to pierce the baffling mists that intervened between his poor purblind eyes and my face, to find some sign of relenting in it.

It was evident that old Major was not happy, in spite of all he had to make him so: although he was well-fed and fat, and treated with the greatest kindness by every one on the place, and although all the other dogs about the house looked up to him with that instinctive respect they always accord to the oldest, or strongest, or most domineering member, his heart was restless and dissatisfied. He could not endure an inactive life. There was, in fact, only one way in which he could or was allowed to work off his superabundant energy. This was when we went down to the river to bathe in the afternoon, and when we would amuse ourselves, some of us, by throwing enormous logs and dead branches into the current. They were large and heavy, and thrown well out into one of the most rapid rivers in the world, but Major would have perished forty times over, if he had had forty lives to throw away, before he would have allowed one of those useless logs to be lost. But this was wasted energy, and Major could not have known it better if he had graduated with honours at the Royal School of Mines, consequently his exertions in the river did not make him happy. His unhappiness began to prey on my mind, and I never left the house but that mute imploring face haunted me for an hour after, until I could bear it no longer. Major conquered, and to witness his boundless delight and gratitude when I shouldered my gun and called him to me, was a pleasure worth many dead birds.

Nothing important happened during our first few expeditions. Major behaved rather wildly, I thought, but he was obedient and anxious to please, and my impression was that he had been too long neglected, and would soon settle down to do his share of the work in a sober, business-like manner.

Then a day came when Major covered himself with glory. I came one morning on a small flock of flamingoes in a lagoon; they were standing in the water, about seventy-five or eighty yards from the shore, quietly dozing. Fortunately the lagoon was bordered by a dense bed of tall rushes, about fifteen yards in breadth, so that I was able to approach the birds unseen by them. I crept up to the rushes in a fever of delighted excitement; not that flamingoes are not common in that district, but because I had noticed that one of the birds before me was the largest and loveliest flamingo I had ever set eyes on, and I had long been anxious to secure one very perfect specimen. I think my hand trembled a great deal; nevertheless, the bird dropped when I fired; and then how quickly the joy I experienced was changed to despair when I looked on the wide expanse of mud, reeds and water that separated him from me! How was I ever to get him? for it is as much as a man's life is worth to venture into one of these long river-like lagoons in the valley, as under the quiet water there is a bed of mire, soft as clotted cream, and deep enough for a giant's grave. I thought of Major, but not

MAJOR AND THE FLAMINGO

for a moment did I believe that he, poor dog! was equal to the task. When I fired he dashed hurriedly forward, and came against the wall of close rushes, where he struggled hopelessly for a little while, and then floundered back to me. There was, however, nothing else to be done. "Major, come here," I called, and, taking a lump of clay I threw it as far as I could towards the floating bird. He raised his ears, and listened to get the right direction, and when the splash of the stone reached us he dashed in and against the rushes once more. After a violent struggle he succeeded in getting through them, and, finding himself in deep water, struck straight out, and then began swimming about in all directions, until, getting to windward of the bird, he followed up the scent and found it. This was the easiest part of the task, as the bird was very large, and when Major got back to the rushes with it, and I heard him crashing and floundering through, snorting and coughing as if half-suffocated, I was sure that if I ever got my flamingo at all it must be hopelessly damaged. At length he appeared, so exhausted with his exertions that he could hardly stand, and deposited the bird at my feet. Never had I seen such a splendid specimen! It was an old cock bird, excessively fat, weighing sixteen pounds, yet Major had brought it out through this slough of despond without breaking its skin, or soiling its exquisitely beautiful crimson, rose-coloured, and faintly-blushing white plumage! Had he not himself been so plastered with mud and slime I should, in gratitude, have taken him into my arms; but he appeared very well satisfied with the words of approval I bestowed on him, and we started homeward in a happy frame of mind, each feeling well pleased with the other—and himself.

That evening as I sat by the fire greatly enjoying my after-dinner coffee, and a pipe of the strongest cavendish, I related the day's adventures, and then for the first time heard from my host some thing of Major's antecedents and remarkable history.

He was a Scotch dog by birth, and had formerly belonged to the Earl of Zetland, and as he proved to be an exceptionally clever and good-looking young dog, he was for a time thought much of; but there was a drop of black blood in Major's heart, and in a moment of temptation it led him into courses for which he was finally condemned to an ignominious death; he escaped to become a pioneer of civilization in the wilderness, and to show even in old age and when his sight had failed him, of what stuff he was made. Killing sheep was his crime; he had hunted the swift-footed cheviots and black faces on the hills and moors; he had tasted their blood and had made the discovery that it was sweet, and the ancient wild dog instinct was hot in his heart. The new joy possessed his whole being, and in a moment swept away every restraint. The savage life was the only real life after all, and what cared Major about the greatest happiness for the greatest number, and new-fangled notions about the division of labour, in which so mean a part was assigned him! Was he to spend a paltry puppy existence retrieving birds, first flushed by a stupid pointer or setter, and shot by a man with a gun—the bird, after all, to be eaten by none of them; and he, in return for his share in the work, to be fed on mild messes and biscuits, and beef, killed somewhere out of sight by a butcher? Away with such a complex state of things! He would not be stifled by such an artificial system; he would kill his own mutton on the moors, and eat it raw and warm in the good old fashion, and enjoy life, as, doubtless, every dog of spirit had enjoyed it a thousand years ago.

This was not to be permitted on a well-conducted estate; and as it was thought that chains and slavery would be less endurable than death to a dog of Major's spirit, to death he was forthwith condemned.

Now it happened that a gentleman, hearing all this from the earl's gamekeeper, before the dread sentence had been executed, all at once remembered that one of his friends, who was preparing to emigrate to Patagonia, purposed taking out some good dogs with him, and thinking that this retriever would form an acceptable gift, he begged for it. The gamekeeper gave it to him, and he in turn gave it to his friend, and in this way Major escaped the penalty, and in due time, after seeing and doubtless reflecting much by the way, arrived at his destination. I say advisably that Major probably reflected a great deal, for in his new home he never once gave way to his criminal appetite for sheep's blood; but whenever the flock came in his way, which was often enough, he turned resolutely aside and skulked off out of the sound of their bleating as quickly as possible.

All I heard from my host only served to raise my opinion of Major, and, remembering what he had accomplished that day, I formed the idea that the most glorious period of his life had just dawned, that he had now begun a series of exploits, compared with which the greatest deeds of all retrievers in other lands would sink into insignificance.

I have now to relate Major's second important exploit, and on this occasion the birds were geese.

The upland geese are excellent eating, and it was our custom to make an early breakfast off a cold goose, or of any remnants left in the larder. Cold boiled goose and coffee, often with no bread—it sounds strange, but never shall I forget those delicious early Patagonian breakfasts.

Now the geese, although abundant at that season, were excessively wary, and hard to kill; and as no other person went after them, although all grumbled loudly when there was no goose for breakfast, I was always very glad to get a shot at them when out with the gun.

One day I saw a great flock congregated on a low mud bank in one of the lagoons, and immediately began to manœuvre to get within shooting distance without disturbing them. Fortunately they were in a great state of excitement, keeping up a loud incessant clamour, as if something very important to the upland geese was being discussed, and in the general agitation they neglected their safety. More geese in small flocks were continually arriving from various directions, increasing the noise and excitement; and by dint of much going on hands and knees and crawling over rough ground, I managed to get within seventy yards of them and fired into the middle of the flock. The birds rose up with a great rush of wings and noise of screams, leaving five of their number floundering about in the shallow water. Major was quickly after them, but two of the five were not badly wounded, and soon swam away beyond his reach; to the others he was guided by the tremendous flapping they made in the water in their death struggles; and one by one he conveyed them, not to his expectant master, but to a small island about a hundred and twenty yards from the shore. No sooner had he got them all together than, to my unspeakable astonishment and dismay, he began worrying them, growling all the time with a playful affectation of anger, and pulling out mouthfuls of feathers which he scattered, in clouds over his head. To my shouts he responded by wagging his tail, and barking a merry crisp little bark, then flying at the dead birds again. He seemed to be telling me, plainly as if he had used words, that he heard me well enough, but was not disposed to obey, that he found it very amusing playing with the geese and intended to enjoy himself to his heart's content.

"Major! Major!" I cried, "you base ungrateful dog! Is this the way you repay me for all my kindness, for befriending you when others spoke evil of you, and made you keep at home, and treated you with contemptuous neglect! Oh, you wretched brute, how many glorious breakfasts are you spoiling with those villainous teeth!"

In vain I stormed and threatened, and told him that I would never speak to him again, that I would thrash him, that I had seen dogs shot for less than what he was doing. I screamed his name until I was hoarse, but it was all useless. Major cared nothing for my shouts, and went on worrying the geese. At length, when he grew tired of his play, he coolly jumped into the water and swam back to me, leaving the geese behind. I waited for him, a stick in my hand, burning for vengeance, and fully intending to collar and thrash him well the moment he reached me. Fortunately he had a long distance to swim, and before he reached land I began to reflect that if I received him roughly, with blows, I would never get the geese—those three magnificent white and maroon-coloured geese that had cost me so much labour to kill. Yes, I thought, it will be better to dissemble and be diplomatic and receive him graciously, and then perhaps he will be persuaded to go again and fetch the geese. In the midst of these plans Major arrived, and sat down facing me without shaking himself, evidently beginning to experience some qualms of conscience.

"Major," said I, addressing him in a mild gentle voice, and patting his wet black head, "you have treated me very badly, but I am not going to punish you—I am going to give you another chance, old dog. Now, Major, good and obedient dog, go and fetch me the geese." With that I pushed him gently towards the water. Major understood me, and went in, although in a somewhat perfunctory manner, and swam back to the island. On reaching it he went up to the geese, examined them briefly with his nose and sat down to deliberate. I called him, but he paid no attention. With what intense anxiety I waited his decision!

At last he appeared to have made up his mind; he stood up, shook himself briskly and—will it be believed?—began to worry the geese again! He was not merely playing with them now, and did not scatter the feathers about and bark, but bit and tore them in a truculent mood. When he had torn them pretty well to pieces he swam back once more, but this time he came to land at a long distance from me, knowing, I suppose, that I was now past speaking mildly to him; and, skulking through the reeds, he sneaked home by himself. Later, when I arrived at the house, he carefully kept out of my way.

I believe that when he went after the geese the second time he really did mean to bring them out, but finding them so much mutilated he thought that he had already hopelessly offended me, and so concluded to save himself the labour of carrying them. He did not know, poor brute, that his fetching them would have been taken as a token of repentance, and that he would have been forgiven. But it was impossible to forgive him now. All faith in him was utterly and for ever gone, and from that day I looked on him as a poor degraded creature; and if I ever bestowed a caress on his upturned face, I did it in the spirit of a man who flings a copper to an unfortunate beggar in the street; and it was a satisfaction to me that Major appeared to know what I thought of him.

But all this happened years ago, and now I can but look with kindly feelings for the old blind retriever who retrieved my geese so badly. I can even laugh at myself for having allowed an ineradicable anthropomorphism to carry me so far in recalling and describing our joint adventures. But such a fault is almost excusable in this instance, for he was really a remarkable dog among other dogs, like a talented man among his fellow-men. I doubt if any other retriever, in such circumstances and handicapped by such an infirmity, could have retrieved that splendid flamingo; but with this excellence there was the innate capacity to go wrong, a sudden reversion to the irresponsible wild dog—the devilry, to keep to human terms, that sent him into exile and made him at the last so interesting and pathetic a figure.

VI

THE WAR WITH NATURE

DURING my sojourn on the Rio Negro letters and papers reached me only at rare intervals. On one occasion I passed very nearly two months without seeing a newspaper. I remember, when at the end of that time one was put before me, I snatched it up eagerly, and began hastily scanning the columns, or column-headings rather, in search of startling items from abroad, and that after a couple of minutes I laid it down again to listen to someone talking in the room, and that I eventually left the place with out reading the paper at all. I suppose I snatched it up at first mechanically, just as a cat, even when not hungry, pounces on a mouse it sees scuttling across its path. It was simply the survival of an old habit—a trick played by unconscious memory on the intellect, like the action of the person who has resided all his life in a hovel, and who, on entering a cathedral door or passing under a lofty archway, unwittingly stoops to avoid bumping his forehead against an imaginary lintel. I was conscious on quitting the room, where I had cast aside the unread newspaper, that the old interest in the affairs of the world at large had in a great measure forsaken me; yet the thought did not seem a degrading one, nor was I at all startled at this newly-discovered indifference, though up till then I had always been profoundly interested in the moves on the great political chessboard of the world. How had I spent those fifty or sixty days, I asked myself, and from what enchanted cup had I drunk the oblivious draught which had wrought so great a change in me? The answer was that I had drunk from the cup of nature, that my days had been spent with peace. It then also seemed to me that the passion for politics, the perpetual craving of the mind for some new thing, is after all only a feverish artificial feeling, a necessary accompaniment of the conditions we live in, perhaps, but from which one rapidly recovers when it can no longer be pandered to, just as a toper, when removed from temptation, recovers a healthy tone of body, and finds to his surprise that he is able to exist without the aid of stimulants. It is easy enough to relapse from this free and pleasant condition; in the latter case the emancipated man goes back to the bottle, in the former to the perusal of leading articles and of the fiery utterances of those who make politics their trade. That I have never been guilty of backsliding I cannot boast; nevertheless the lesson nature taught me in that lonely country was not wholly wasted, and while I was in that condition of mind I found it very agreeable. I was delighted to discover that the stimulus derived from many daily telegrams and much discussion of remote probabilities were not necessary to keep my mind from lethargy. Things about which I had hitherto cared little now occupied my thoughts and supplied me with pleasurable excitement. How fresh and how human it seemed to feel a keen interest in the village annals, the domestic life, the simple pleasures, cares, and struggles of the people I lived with! This is a feeling only to be experienced in any great degree by the soul that has ceased to vex itself with the ambitious schemes of Russia, the attitude of the Sublime Porte, and the meeting or breaking up of parliaments. When the Eastern Question had lost its ancient fascination for me I found a world large enough for my sympathies in the little community of men and women on the Rio Negro. Here for upwards of a century the colony has existed, cut off, as it were, by hundreds of desert leagues from all communion with fellow-christians, surrounded by a great wilderness, waterless and overgrown with thorns, peopled only by pumas, ostriches, and wandering tribes of savage men. In this romantic isolation the colonists spend their whole lives, roaming in childhood over the wooded uplands; in after life with one cloud always on their otherwise sunlit horizon—the fear of the red man, and always ready to fly to arms and mount their horses when the cannon booms forth its loud alarm from the fort.

It must of necessity have been a case of war to the knife with these white aliens—war not only with the wild tribes that cherish an undying feud against the robbers of their inheritance, but also with Nature. For when man begins to cultivate the soil, to introduce domestic cattle, and to slay a larger number of wild animals than he requires for food—and civilized man must do all that to create the conditions he imagines necessary to his existence—from that moment does he place himself in antagonism with Nature, and has thereafter to suffer countless persecutions at her hands. After a century of residence in the valley the colonist has established his position so that he cannot be driven out. Twenty-five years ago it was still possible for a great cacique to gallop into the town, clattering his silver harness and flourishing his spear, to demand with loud threats of vengeance his unpaid annual tribute of cattle, knife-blades, indigo, and cochineal. Now the red man's spirit is broken; in numbers and in courage he is declining. During the last decade the desert places have been abundantly watered with his blood, and, before many years are over, the old vendetta will be forgotton, for he will have ceased to exist.

Nature, albeit now without his aid, still maintains the conflict, enlisting the elements, with bird, beast, and insect, against the hated white disturber, whose way of life is not in harmony with her way.

There are the animal foes. Pumas infest the settlement. At all seasons a few of these sly but withal audacious robbers haunt the riverside; but in winter a great many lean and hungry individuals come down from the uplands to slay the sheep and horses, and it is extremely difficult to track them to their hiding places in the thorny thickets overhanging the valley. I was told that not less than a hundred pumas were killed annually by the shepherds and herdsmen. The depredations of the locusts are on a much larger scale. In summer I frequently rode over miles of ground where they literally carpeted the earth with their numbers, rising in clouds before me, causing a sound as of a loud wind with their wings. It was always the same, I was told; every year they appeared at some point in the valley to destroy the crops and pasturage. Then there were birds of many species and in incalculable numbers. To an idle sportsman without a stake in the country it was paradise. At one spot I noticed all the wheat ruined, most of the stalks being stripped and broken, presenting a very curious appearance; I was surprised to hear from the owner of the desolate fields that in this instance the coots had been the culprits. Thousands of these birds came up from the river every night, and in spite of all he could do to frighten them away they had succeeded in wasting his corn.

On either side of the long straggling settlement spreads the uninhabited desert—uninhabitable, in fact, for it is waterless, with a sterile gravelly soil that only produces a thorny vegetation of dwarf trees. It serves, however, as a breeding-place for myriads of winged creatures; and never a season passes but it sends down its hungry legions of one kind or another into the valley. During my stay pigeons, ducks, and geese were the greatest foes of the farmer. When the sowing season commenced the pigeons (*Columba maculosa*) came in myriads to devour the grain, which is here sown broadcast. Shooting and poisoning them was practised on some farms, while on others dogs were trained to hunt the birds from the ground; but notwithstanding all these measures, half the seed committed to the earth was devoured. When the corn was fully ripe and ready to be harvested then came the brown duck (*Dafila spinacauda*) in millions to feast on the grain. Early in winter the arrival of the migratory upland geese (*Chloephaga magellanica*) was dreaded. It is scarcely possible to keep them from the fields when the wheat is young or just beginning to sprout; and I have frequently seen flocks of these birds quietly feeding under the very shadow of the fluttering scarecrows set up to frighten them. They do even greater injury to the pasture-lands, where they are often so numerous as to denude the earth of the tender young clover, thus depriving the sheep of their only food. On some estates mounted boys were kept scouring the plains, and driving up the flocks with loud shouts; but their labours were quite profitless; fresh armies of geese on their way north were continually pouring in, making a vast camping ground of the valley, till scarcely a blade of grass remained for the perishing cattle.

Viewed from a distance, in comfortable homes, this contest of man with the numberless destructive forces of nature is always looked on as the great drawback in the free life of the settler—the drop of bitter in the cup which spoils its taste. It is a false notion, although it would no doubt be upheld as true by most of those who are actually engaged in the contest, and should know. This is strange, but not unaccountable. Our feelings become modified and changed altogether with regard to many things as we progress in life, and experience widens, but in most cases the old expressions are still used. We continue to call black black, because we were taught so, and have always called it black, although it may now seem purple or blue or some other colour. We learn a kind of emasculated language in the nursery, from schoolmasters, and books written indoors, and it has to serve us. It proves false, but its falsity is perhaps never clearly recognized; Nature emancipates us and the feeling changes, but there has been no conscious reasoning on the matter, and thought is vague. One hears a person relating the struggles and storms of his early or past life, and receiving without protest expressions of sympathy and pity from his listeners; but he knows in his heart, albeit his brain may be and generally is in a mist, that these were the very things that exhilarated him, that if he had missed them his life would have been savourless. For the healthy man, or for the man whose virile instincts have not become atrophied in the artificial conditions we exist in, strife of some kind, if not physical then mental, is essential to happiness. It is a principle of Nature that only by means of strife can strength be maintained. No sooner is any species placed above it, or over-protected, than degeneration begins. But about the condition of the inferior animals, with regard to the comparative dulness or brightness of their lives, we do not concern ourselves. It is pleasant to be able to believe that they are all in a sense happy, although hard to believe that they are happy in the same degree. The sloth, for instance, that most over-protected mammalian, fast asleep as he hugs his branch, and the wild cat that has to save himself, and must for ever and always keep all his faculties keen and brightly polished. With regard to man, who has the power of self-analysis and of seeing in his own mind all minds, the case is very different, and it does concern us to know the truth. A great deal—very many pages, chapters and even books—might be written on this subject, but to write them is happily unnecessary, since every one can easily find out the truth from his own experience. This will tell him which satisfied him most in the end—the rough days or the smooth in his life; and which was most highly valued—the good he struggled for or that which came to him in some other way. Even as a child, or as a small boy, assuming that his early years were passed in fairly natural conditions, the knocks and bruises and scratches and stings of infuriated bumble-bees he suffered served only to excite a spirit that had something of conscious power and gladness in it; and in this the child was father to the man. But the subject which specially concerns me just now is the settler's life in some new and rough district; and as it appears that the greatest, the most real, and in many cases the only pleasures of such an existence are habitually spoken of as pains, the subject is one on which I may be pardoned for dwelling at some length.

If Mill's doctrine be true, that all our happiness results from delusion, that to one capable of seeing things as they are life must be an intolerable burden, then it may seem only a cruel kindness to whisper into the ear of the emigrant the warning—"That which thou goes forth to seek thou shalt not find."

It is not said, be it remembered, that he will not find happiness, which, like the rain and sunshine, although in more moderate measure, comes alike to all men; it is only said that the particular form of happiness to which he looks forward will never be his. But one need not fear to whisper the warning, nor even to shout it from the house-tops, for, to begin with, he will not believe nor listen to it. His mind is fixed on the three glorious prizes that lure him away—Adventure, Distinction, Gold. These bright and shining apples are perhaps just as common at home as abroad, and as easily gathered; but the young enthusiast, surveying coasts five or ten thousand miles away through his mental telescope, sees them apparently hanging on very much lower branches, and imagines that to pluck them he has only to transport himself beyond the ocean. To drop this metaphor, adventure in that distant place will be as common as the air he breathes, giving him much invigorating pleasure by the way, while he advances to possess himself of other more satisfying things. With the nimble brains, brave spirit, and willing hands characteristic of the inhabitants of the British Islands, he will assuredly be able to achieve distinction—that pretty bit of ribbon which most men are willing enough to wear.

This, however, is only a matter of secondary importance; the chief prize will always be the yellow metal. Knowing how much can be done with it at home where it is held in great esteem, he will take care to provide himself with an abundant supply against his return. The precise way in which it is to be acquired he will not trouble himself about until he reaches his destination. It will perhaps flow in upon him through business channels; in most cases it will be thought more agreeable to pick it up in its native state during his walks abroad in the forest. The simple-minded aborigines, always ready to humour an eccentric taste, will assist him in collecting it; and, finally, for a small consideration in the form of coloured beads and pocket-mirrors, convey it in large sacks and hampers to the place of embarkation. It is not meant that the immigrant in all cases paints his particular delusion in colours bright as these; let him shade the picture until it corresponds in tone with his individual creation—a dream and a delusion it will nevertheless remain. Not in these things which will never be his, nor in still cherishing the dream will he find his pleasure, but in something very different.

I speak not of that large percentage of immigrants who are doomed to find no pleasure at all, and no good. To the youth of ardent generous temperament, arrived in some far-off city where all men are free and equal, and the starched conventionalities of the old world are unknown, it is perhaps the hardest thing to believe that when he slips down not a hand will be put forth to raise him; that when he pronounces these common words, "I have come to the end of my tether," instantly all the smiling faces surrounding him will vanish as if by magic; that the few sovereigns remaining in his pocket at any time are as a chain, shortened each day by a link, holding him back from some terrible destiny…Let us delay no longer in this moral place of skulls, but follow that wise, and sturdy youth who, wrapping his cloak about his face, passes unharmed through the poisonous atmosphere of the landing-place, and hurries a thousand miles away, while ever

> Before him, like a blood-red flag,

flutters and shines the dream that lures him on. And now at his journey's end comes reality to lay rude hands on him with rough shaking. Meanwhile, before he has quite recovered from the shock, that red flag on which his dreamy eyes have been so long fixed stays not, but travels on and on to disappear at last like a sunset cloud in the distant horizon. He does not miss it greatly after all. The actual is much in his thoughts. When a man is buffeting the waves he does not curiously examine the landscape before him and complain that there are no bright flowers on the trees. New experience takes the place of vanished dreams, which, like water-lilies, blossom only on stagnant pools. Here are none of the innumerable appliances to secure comfort he has been used to from infancy, regarding them almost as spontaneous productions of the earth; no hand to perform a hundred necessary offices, so that this dainty gentleman is obliged to blacken his own boots, tame and harness to the plough his own bullocks or horses, kill and cook his own mutton. Nothing is here, in fact, but harsh Nature reluctant to be subdued; while he, to subdue her and make his own conditions, has only a pair of soft weak hands.

To one fresh from the softness and smoothness of civilization, unaccustomed to manual labour, how hard then is the lot of the settler! Behind him physical comfort and beautiful dreams; before him the prospect of long years of unremitting toil, every day of which will unfit him more and more for a return to the gentle life of the past; while, for only result, he will have food enough to satisfy hunger, and a rude shelter from extremes of heat and cold, from torrents of winter rain and blinding clouds of summer dust. Yet is he happy. For the vanished substantial comforts and airy splendours there is a compensation gilding his rough existence with a better brightness than that of any hope of future prosperity which may yet linger in his mind. It is the feeling the settler experiences from the moment of his induction into the desert that he is engaged in a conflict, and there is no feeling comparable with it to put a man on his mettle and inspire him with a healthy and enduring interest in life. To this feeling is added the charm of novelty caused by that endless procession of surprises which nature prepares for the pioneer—an experience unknown to the rural life of countries that have long been under cultivation. The greatest drawbacks and difficulties encountered have this charm strongest in them, and are robbed by it of half their power to discourage the mind.

The young enthusiast, hurrying about London to speak his farewells and look after his outfit, will perhaps laugh at this, for his delusion is still dear to him. But I am not discouraging him; I am, on the contrary, telling him of a rill of pure water out there where he is going, where, for many years to come, he will refresh himself every day, and learn to feel (if not to think and to say) that it is the sweetest rill in existence.

It is rough living with unsubdued, or only partially subdued, Nature, but there is a wonderful fascination in it. The patient, leaden-footed, but always obedient drudge, who goes forth uncomplainingly, albeit often with a sullen face, about her work, day after day, year after year; who never rebels, never murmurs against her bad task-master Man, although sometimes the strength fails her so that she cannot complete the appointed task—this is Nature at home in England. How strange to see this stolid, immutable creature transformed beyond the seas into a flighty, capricious thing, that will not be wholly ruled by you, a beautiful wayward Undine, delighting you with her originality, and most lovable when she teases most; a being of extremes, always either in laughter or tears, a tyrant and a slave alternately; to-day shattering to pieces the work of yesterday; now cheerfully doing more than is required of her; anon the frantic vixen that buries her malignant teeth into the hand that strikes or caresses her. All these rapid incomprehensible changes, even when most vexing and destructive to your plans, interest your mind, and call up a hundred latent energies it is a joy to discover. But you have not yet sounded all her depths; nor can you imagine, seeing her frequent gay smiles, to what length her fierce resentment may carry her. Sometimes, as if roused to sudden frenzy at the indignities you are subjecting her to—hacking at her trees, turning up her cushioned soil, and trampling down her grass and flowers—she arrays herself in her blackest, most terrible aspect, and like a beautiful woman who in her fury has no regard for her beauty, she plucks up her noblest trees by the roots, and scooping up the very soil from the earth whirls it aloft to give a more horrible gloom to the heavens. And darkness not being terrifying enough, she kindles up the mighty chaos she has created into a blaze of intolerable light, while the solid world is shaken to its foundations with her wrathful thunders. When destruction seems about to fall on man and all his works, when you are prostrate and ready to perish with excessive fear, lo, the mood changes, the furious passion has spent itself, and there is no trace left of it when you look up only to encounter her peaceful reassuring smile. These sublime moods are, however, infrequent and soon forgotten; man learns to despise the threats of a cataclysm that never comes, and goes forth once more to level the ancient trees, to invert the soil, and pasture his herds on her grasses and flowers. He will subdue the wild thing at last, but not yet; many years will she struggle to retain her ancient sweet supremacy; he cannot alter all at once the old order to which she clings tenaciously, as the red man to his savage life. Her attempt to frighten him away has failed. He laughs at her mask of terrors—he knows that it is only a mask; and it suffocates her and cannot be long endured. She will cast it aside and fight him another way. She will stoop to his yoke and be docile only to betray and defeat him at the last. A thousand strange tricks and surprises will she invent to molest him. In a hundred forms she will buzz in his ears and prick his flesh with stings; she will sicken him with the perfume of flowers, and poison him with sweet honey; and when he lies down to rest, she will startle him with the sudden apparition of a pair of lidless eyes and a flickering forked tongue. He scatters the seed, and when he looks for the green heads to appear, the earth opens, and lo, an army of long-faced, yellow grasshoppers come forth! She, too, walking invisible at his side, had scattered her miraculous seed along with his. He will not be beaten by her, he slays her striped and spotted creatures; he dries up her marshes; he consumes her forests and prairies with fire, and her wild things perish in myriads; he covers her plains with herds of cattle, and waving fields of corn, and orchards of fruit-bearing trees. She hides her bitter wrath in her heart, secretly she goes out at dawn of day and blows her trumpet on the hills, summoning her innumerable children to her aid. She is hard-pressed and cries to her children that love her to come and deliver her. Nor are they slow to hear. From north and south, from east and west, they come in armies of creeping things and in clouds that darken the air. Mice and crickets swarm in the fields; a thousand insolent birds pull his scarecrows to pieces, and carry off the straw stuffing to build their nests; every green thing is devoured; the trees, stripped of their bark, stand like great white skeletons in the bare desolate fields, cracked and scorched by the pitiless sun. When he is in despair deliverance comes; famine falls on the mighty host of his enemies; they devour each other and perish utterly. Still he lives to lament his loss; to strive still, unsubdued and resolute. She, too, laments her lost children, which now, being dead, serve only to fertilize the soil and give fresh strength to her implacable enemy. And she, too, is unsubdued; she dries her tears and laughs again; she has found out a new weapon it will take him long to wrest from her hands. Out of many little humble plants she fashions the mighty noxious weeds; they spring up in his footsteps, following him everywhere, and possess his fields like parasites, sucking up their moisture and killing their fertility. Everywhere, as if by a miracle, is spread the mantle of rich, green, noisome leaves, and the corn is smothered in beautiful flowers that yield only bitter seed and poison fruit. He may cut them down in the morning, in the night time they will grow again. With her beloved weeds she will wear out his spirit and break his heart; she will sit still at a distance and laugh while he grows weary of the hopeless struggle; and, at last, when he is ready to faint,

UPLAND GEESE

she will go forth once more and blow her trumpet on the hills and call her innumerable children to come and fall on and destroy him utterly.

This is no mere fancy portrait, for Nature herself sat for it in the desert, and it is painted in true colours. Such is the contest the settler embarks in—so various in its fortunes, so full of great and sudden vicissitudes, calling for so much vigilance and strategy on his part. If the dreams he sets out with are never realized, he is no worse off in this respect than others. To one, born and bred on the plains, the distant mountain range is ever a region of enchantment; when he reaches it the glory is no more; the opalescent tints and blue ethereal shadows of noon, the violet hues of the sunset have vanished. There is nothing after all but a rude confusion of piled rocks; but although this is not what he expected, he ends by preferring the mountain's roughness to the monotony of the plain. The man who finishes his course by a fall from his horse, or is swept away and drowned when fording a swollen stream, has, in most cases, spent a happier life than he who dies of apoplexy in a counting-house or dining-room; or, who, finding that end which seemed so infinitely beautiful to Leigh Hunt (which to me seems so unutterably hateful), drops his white face on the open book before him. Certainly he has been less world-weary, and has never been heard to whine and snivel about the vanity of all things.

VII

LIFE IN PATAGONIA

FROM the dribbling warfare described in the last chapter, with clouds of winged things for principal enemy, let us go back once more to that sterner conflict with hostile men, in which the isolated little colony has so often been involved during its century of existence. One episode from its eventful history I wish to relate, for in this instance the Patagonians had, for once, to oppose a foreign and civilized foe. The story is so strange, even in the romantic annals of South America, as to seem almost incredible. The main facts are, however, to be found in historical documents. The details given here were taken from the lips of persons living on the spot, and who had been familiar with the story from childhood.

Very early in this century the Brazilians became convinced that in the Argentine nation they had a determined foe to their aggressive and plundering policy, and for many years they waged war against Buenos Ayres, putting forth all their feeble energies in operations by land and sea to crush their troublesome neighbour, until 1828, when they finally abandoned the contest. During this war the Imperialists conceived the idea of capturing the Patagonian settlement of El Carmen, which they knew to be quite unprotected. Three ships of war, with a large number of soldiers, were sent out to effect this insignificant conquest, and in due time reached the Rio Negro. One of the ships came to grief on the bar, which is very difficult; and there it eventually became a total wreck. The other two succeeded in getting safely into the river. The troops, to the number of 500 men, were disembarked and sent on to capture the town, which is twenty miles distant from the sea. The ships at the same time proceeded up the river, though it was scarcely thought that their co-operation would be required to take so weak a place as the Carmen. Happily for the colonists, the Imperial armada found the navigation difficult, and one of the ships ran on to a sandbank about half-way to the town; the other proceeded alone only to arrive when it was all over with the land force. This force, finding it impossible to continue its march near the river, owing to the steep hills intersected by valleys and ravines and covered with a dense forest of thorns, was compelled to take a circuitous route leading it several miles away from the water.

Tidings of the approaching army soon reached the Carmen, and all able-bodied men within call were quickly mustered in the fort. They numbered only seventy, but the Patagonians were determined to defend themselves. Women and children were brought into the fort; guns were loaded and placed in position; then the commander had a happy inspiration, and all the strong women were made to display themselves on the walls in male attire. Dummy soldiers, hastily improvised from blocks of wood, bolsters, and other materials, were also placed at intervals; so that when the Brazilians arrived in sight they were surprised to see four or five hundred men, as they thought, on the ramparts before them. From the high ground behind the town where they had halted they commanded a view of the river for several miles, but the expected ships were not yet in sight. The day had been oppressively hot, without a cloud, and that march of about thirty miles over the waterless desert had exhausted the men. Probably they had been suffering from sea-sickness during the voyage; at any rate, they were now mad with thirst, worn out, and not in a fit state to attack a position seemingly so strongly defended. They determined to retire, and wait for a day or two, and then attack the place in concert with the ships. To the joy and amazement of the Patagonians, their formidable enemy left without firing a shot. Another happy inspiration came to the aid of the commander, and as soon as the Brazilians had disappeared behind the rising ground, his seventy men were hastily dispatched to collect and bring in all the horses pasturing in the valley. When the invaders had been about three or four hours on their spiritless return march, the thunder of innumerable hoofs was heard behind them, and looking back, they beheld a great army, as they imagined in their terror, charging down upon them. These were their seventy foes spread in an immense half-moon, in the hollow of which over a thousand horses were being driven along at frantic speed. The Brazilians received their equine enemy with a discharge of musketry; but though many horses were slain or wounded, the frantic yells of the drivers behind still urged them on, and in a few moments, blind with panic, they were trampling down the invaders. In the meantime the Patagonians were firing into the confused mass of horses and men; and by a singular chance—a miracle it was held to be at the time—the officer commanding the Imperial troops was shot dead by a stray bullet; then the men threw down their arms and surrendered at discretion—500 disciplined soldiers of the Empire to seventy poor Patagonians, mostly farmers, tradesmen, and artisans. The honour of the Empire was very little to those famishing wretches crying out with frothing mouths for water instead of quarter. Leaving their muskets scattered about the plain, they were marched by their captors down to the river, which was about four miles off, and reached it at a point just where the bank slopes down between the Parrot's Cliff on one side, and the house I resided in on the other. Like a herd of cattle maddened with thirst, they rushed into the water, trampling each other down in their haste, so that many were smothered, while others, pushed too far out by the surging mass behind, were swept from their feet by the swift current and drowned. When they had drunk their fill, they were driven like cattle to the Carmen and shut up within the fort. In the evening the ship arrived before the town, and, going a little too near the shore on the opposite side, ran aground. The men in her were quickly apprised of the disaster which had overtaken the land force; meanwhile the resolute Patagonians, concealed amongst the trees on the shore, began to pepper the deck with musket-balls; the Brazilians, in terror for their lives, leaped into the water and swam to land; and when darkness fell, the colonists had crowned their brave day's work by the capture of the Imperial war-vessel *Itaparica*. No doubt it was soon pulled to pieces, good building material being rather expensive on the Rio Negro; a portion of the wreck, however, still lies in the river, and often, when the tide was low, and those old brown timbers came up above the surface, like the gaunt fossil ribs of some gigantic Pliocene monster, I have got out of my boat and stood upon them experiencing a feeling of great satisfaction. Thus the awful war-cloud burst, and the little colony, by pluck and cunning and readiness to strike at the proper moment, saved itself from the disgrace of being conquered by the infamous Empire of the tropics.

During my residence at the house alongside the Parrot's Cliff, one of our neighbours I was very much interested in was a man named Sosa. He was famed for an almost preternatural keenness of sight, had great experience of the wild life of the frontier, and was always employed as a scout in times of Indian warfare. He was also a celebrated horse-thief. His horse-stealing propensities were ineradicable, and had to be winked at on account of his usefulness; so that he was left in a great measure to his own devices. He was, in fact, a fox hired to act as watch-dog to the colony in times of danger; and though the victims of his numberless thefts had always been anxious to wreak personal vengeance on him, his vulpine sagacity had so far enabled him to escape them all. My interest in him arose from the fact that he was the son of a man whose name figures in Argentine history. Sosa's father was an illiterate gaucho—a man of the plains—possessing faculties so keen that to ordinary beings his feats of vision and hearing, and his sense of direction on the monotonous pampas, seemed almost miraculous. As he also possessed other qualities suitable to a leader of men in a semi-savage region, he rose in time to the command of the south-western frontier, where his numerous victories over the Indians gave him so great a prestige that the jealousy of the Dictator Rosas—the Nero of South America, as he was called by his enemies—was roused, and at his instigation Sosa was removed by means of a cup of poison. The son, though in all other respects a degenerate being, inherited his father's wonderful senses. One instance of his keen sightedness which I heard struck me as very curious. In 1861 Sosa had found it prudent to disappear for a season from the colony in the company of five or six more gauchos—also offenders against the law, who had flown to the refuge of the desert—he amused himself by hunting ostriches along the Rio Colorado. On the 12th of March the hunters were camping beside a grove of willows in the valley, and about nine o'clock that evening, while seated round the fire roasting their ostrich meat, Sosa suddenly sprang to his feet and held his open hand high above his head for some moments. "There is not a breath of wind blowing," he exclaimed, "yet the leaves of the trees are trembling. What can this portend?" The others stared at the trees, but could see no motion, and began to laugh and jeer at him. Presently he sat down again, remarking that the trembling had ceased; but during the rest of the evening he seemed very much disturbed in his mind. He remarked repeatedly that such a thing had never happened in his experience before, for, he said, he could feel a breath of wind before the leaves felt it, and there had been no wind; he feared that it was a warning of some disaster about to overtake their party. The disaster was not for them. On that evening, when Sosa sprang up terrified and pointed to the leaves which to the others appeared motionless, occurred the earthquake which destroyed the distant city of Mendoza, crushing twelve thousand people to death in its fall. That the subterranean wave extended east to the Plata, and southwards into Patagonia, was afterwards known, for in the cities of Rosario and Buenos Ayres clocks stopped, and a slight shock was also experienced in the Carmen on the Rio Negro.

My host, whose Christian name was Ventura, being a Patagonian by birth, and not far off fifty years old, must, I imagined, have seen a thousand things worth relating, and I frequently importuned him to tell some of his early experiences in the settlement. But somehow he invariably drifted into amorous and gambling reminiscences, interesting in their way, some of them, but they were not the kind of recollections I wished to hear. The empire of his affections had been divided between Cupid and cards; and apparently everything he had seen or experienced in fifty eventful years, unless it had some relation to one of the two divinities, was clean forgotten—cast away from him like the ends of the innumerable cigarettes he had been smoking all his life. Once, however, a really interesting adventure of his boyhood was recalled accidentally to his mind. He came home one evening from the Carmen, where he had been spending the day, and during supper told me the following story.

When he was about sixteen years old he was sent one day with four others— three lads like himself, and a middle-aged man named Marcos in charge of them—with a herd of horses required for military service at a place twenty-five leagues up the river. For, at that period, every person was at the beck and call of the commander of the colony. Half-way to their destination there was a corral, or cattle-enclosure, standing two or three hundred yards from the river, but miles away from any habitation. They drove their animals into the corral, and, after

DAMIAN GIVES HIMSELF UP

unsaddling and turning loose the beasts they had ridden, were about to catch fresh horses, when a troop of Indians was spied charging down upon them. "Follow me, boys!" shouted Marcos, for there was no time to lose, and away they rushed to the river, throwing off their clothes as they ran. In a few moments they were in the water swimming for life, the shouts of the savages ringing in their ears. The river at this point was about eight hundred feet broad, with a strong current, and two of the lads dared not venture across, but escaped, diving and swimming along under the shadow of the bank like a couple of water-rats or wounded ducks, and finally concealed themselves in a reed bed at some distance. The others, led by Marcos, being good swimmers like most of the Patagonians, struck boldly out for the opposite shore. But when they approached it and were beginning to congratulate themselves on their escape, they were suddenly confronted with another party of mounted Indians, standing a few yards back from the margin and quietly waiting their arrival. They turned and swam away to the middle of the stream once more: here one of them, a youth named Damian, began to exclaim that he was getting tired, and would sink unless Marcos would save him. Marcos told him to save himself if he could; then Damian, bitterly reproaching him for his selfishness, declared that he would swim back to the side they had started from and give himself up to the Indians. Naturally they made no objection, being unable to help him and so Damian left them, and when the Indians saw him approaching they got off their horses and came down to the margin, their lances in their hands. Of course Damian knew right well that savages seldom burden themselves with a male captive when they happen to be out on the war-path; but he was a clever boy, and though death by steel was more painful than death by drowning, there was still a faint chance that his captors might have compassion on him. He began, in fact, to appeal to their mercy from the moment he abandoned his companions. "Indians! friends! brothers!" he shouted aloud from the water. "Do not kill me: in heart I am an Indian like one of yourselves, and no Christian. My skin is white, I know; but I hate my own race, to escape from them has always been my one desire. To live with the Indians I love, in the desert, that is the only wish of my heart. Spare me, brothers, take me with you, and I will serve you all my life. Let me live with you, hunt with you, fight with you—especially against the hated Christians."

In the middle of the river Marcos lifted up his face and laughed hoarsely to hear this eloquent address; though they expected to see poor Damian thrust through with spears the very next moment, he could not help laughing. They watched him arrive, still loudly crying out for mercy, astonishing them very much with his oratorical powers, for Damian had not hitherto made any display of this kind of talent. The Indians took him by the hands and drew him out of the water, then, surrounding him, walked him away to the corral, and from that moment Damian disappeared from the valley; for on a search being made afterwards, not even his bones, picked clean by vultures and foxes, could be found.

After seeing the last of their comrade, and keeping themselves afloat with the least possible exertion, Marcos and Ventura were carried down the stream by the swift current till they gained a small island in the middle of the river. With the drift-wood found on it they constructed a raft, binding the sticks together with long grass and rushes, and on it they floated downstream to the inhabited portion of the valley, and so eventually made their escape.

The reason why my host told me this story instead of one of his usual love intrigues or gambling adventures was because that very day he had seen Damian once more, just returned to the settlement where he had so long been forgotten by everyone. Thirty years of exposure to the sun and wind of the desert had made him so brown, while in manner and speech he had grown so like an Indian, that the poor amateur savage found it hard at first to establish his identity. His relations had, however, been poor, and had long passed away, leaving nothing for him to inherit, so that there was no reason to discredit his strange story. He related that when the Indians drew him from the water and carried him back to the corral they disagreed among themselves as to what they should do to him. Luckily one of them understood Spanish, and translated to the others the substance of Damian's speech delivered from the water. When they questioned their captive he invented many other ingenious lies, saying that he was a poor orphan boy, and that the cruel treatment his master subjected him to had made him resolve to escape to the Indians. The only feeling he had towards his own race, he assured them, was one of undying animosity; and he was ready to vow that if they would only let him join their tribe he would always be ready for a raid on the Christian settlement. To see the entire white race swept away with fire and steel was, in fact, the cherished hope of his heart. Their savage breasts were touched with his piteous tale of sufferings; his revengeful feelings were believed to be genuine, and they took him to their own home, where he was permitted to share in the simple delights of the aborigines. They belonged to a tribe very powerful at that time, inhabiting a district called Las Manzanas—that is, the Apple Country—situated at the sources of the Rio Negro in the vicinity of the Andes.

There is a tradition that shortly after the conquest of South America a few courageous Jesuit priests crossed over from Chili to the eastern slopes of the Andes to preach Christianity to the tribes there, and that they took with them implements of husbandry, grain, and seeds of European fruits. The missionaries soon met death, and all that remained of their labours among the heathen were a few apple-trees they had planted. These trees found a soil and climate so favourable, that they soon began to propagate spontaneously, becoming exceedingly abundant. Certain it is that now, after two or three centuries of neglect by man, these wild apple-trees still yield excellent fruit, which the Indians eat, and from which they also make a fermented liquor they call *chi-chi*.

To this far-off fertile region Damian was taken to lead the kind of life he professed to love. Here were hill, forest, and clear swift river, great undulating plains, the pleasant pasture-lands of the huanaco, ostrich, and wild horse; and beyond all in the west the stupendous mountain range of the Cordilleras—a realm of enchantment and ever-changing beauty. Very soon, however, when the novelty of the new life had worn off, together with the exultation he had experienced at his escape from cruel death, his heart began to be eaten up with secret grief, and he pined for his own people again. Escape was impossible: to have revealed his true feelings would have exposed him to instant cruel death. To take kindly to the savage way of life, outwardly at least, was now his only course. With cheerful countenance he went forth on long hunting expeditions in the depth of winter, exposed all day to bitter cold and furious storms of wind and sleet, cursed and beaten for his awkwardness by his fellow huntsmen; at night stretching his aching limbs on the wet stony ground, with the rug they permitted him to wear for only covering. When the hunters were unlucky it was customary to slaughter a horse for food. The wretched animal would be first drawn up by its hind legs and suspended from the branches of a great tree, so that all the blood might be caught, for this is the chief delicacy of the Patagonian savage. An artery would be opened in the neck and the spouting blood caught in large earthen vessels; then, when the savages gathered round to the feast, poor Damian would be with them to drink his share of the abhorred liquid, hot from the heart of the still living brute. In autumn, when the apples were fermented in pits dug in the earth and lined with horse hides to prevent the juice from escaping, he would take part, as became a true savage, in the grand annual drinking bouts. The women would first go round carefully gathering up all knives, spears, bolas, or other weapons dangerous in the hands of drunken men, to carry them away into the forest, where they would conceal themselves with the children. Then for days the warriors would give themselves up to the joys of intoxication; and at such times unhappy Damian would come in for a large share of ridicule, blows, and execrations; the Indians being full of boisterous fun or else truculent in their cups, and loving above all things to have a *Kokó-huinché*, or "white fool" for a butt.

At length, when he came to man's estate, was fluent in their language, and outwardly in all things like a savage, a wife was bestowed on him, and she bore him several children. Those he had first known as grown up or old men gradually died off, were killed, or drifted away; children who had always known Damian as one of the tribe grew to manhood, and it was forgotten that he had ever been a Christian and a captive. Yet still, with his helpmate by his side, weaving rugs and raiment for him or ministering to his wants—for the Indian wife is always industrious and the patient, willing, affectionate slave of her lord—and with all his young barbarians at play on the grass before his hut, he would sit in the waning sunlight oppressed with sorrow, dreaming the old dreams he could not banish from his heart. And at last, when his wife began to grow wrinkled and dark-skinned, as a middle-aged Indian mother invariably does, and when his children were becoming men, the gnawing discontent at his breast made him resolve to leave the tribe and the life he secretly hated. He joined a hunting-party going towards the Atlantic coast, and after travelling for some days with them his opportunity came, when he secretly left them and made his way alone to the Carmen.

"And there he is," concluded Ventura, when he had told the story, with undisguised contempt for Damian in his tone, "an Indian and nothing less! Does he imagine he can ever be like one of us after living that life for thirty years? If Marcos were alive, how he would laugh to see Damian back again, sitting cross-legged on the floor, solemn as a cacique, brown as old leather, and calling himself a white man! Yet here he says he will remain, and here amongst Christians he will die. Fool, why did he not escape twenty years ago, or, having remained so long in the desert, why has he now come back where he is not wanted!"

Ventura was very unsympathetic, and appeared to have no kindly feelings left for his old companion-in-arms, but I was touched with the story I had heard. There was something pathetic in the life of that poor returned wanderer, an alien now to his own fellow-townsmen, homeless amidst the pleasant vineyards, poplar groves, and old stone houses where he had first seen the light; listening to the bells from the church tower as he had listened to them in childhood, and perhaps for the first time realizing in a dull vague kind of way that it might never more be with him as it had been in the vanished past. Possibly also, the memory of his savage spouse who had loved him many years would add some

DAMIAN'S WIFE

bitterness to his strange isolated life. For, far away in their old home, she would still wait for him, vainly hoping, fearing much, dim-eyed with sorrow and long watching, yet never seeing his form returning to her out of the mysterious haze of the desert!

Poor Damian, and poor wife!

VIII

SNOW, AND THE QUALITY OF WHITENESS

IN August, the April of the Argentine poets, we had some piercingly cold weather, followed by a fall of snow. Heaven be praised for it! for never again, perhaps, shall I see earth transfigured by the breath of antarctic winter. I had spent the night in the village, and it was a strange and weirdly beautiful sight, when, on rising next morning, I beheld roads, housetops, trees, and the adjacent hills, white with a surpassing unfamiliar whiteness. The morning was mild, with a dull leaden sky; and suddenly, as I stood in the street, the snow began to fall again, and continued for about an hour. Most of that time I spent standing motionless, gazing up into the air, peopled with innumerable large slow-descending flakes: only those of my English readers who, like Kingsley, have longed for a sight of tropical vegetation and scenery, and have *at last* had their longing gratified, can appreciate my sensations on first beholding snow.

My visit to Patagonia so far had been rich in experiences. One of the first, just before touching its shores, but after the ship had struck on the hidden rocks, was the effect of whiteness as seen in a tumultuous milky sea; and now, after several months, there came this snow-fall, and a vaster and stranger whiteness. My uppermost feeling at the time was one of delight at seeing what I had been hoping for months to see, but had now, when winter was so nearly over, ceased to hope for. This pleasure was purely intellectual; but when I ask myself if there was anything besides, a deeper, undefinable feeling, I can only answer, I think not: my first experience of snow does not lead me to believe that there is any instinctive feeling in us related to it; that the feeling which so many, perhaps a majority of persons, experience on seeing the earth whitened by the breath of winter, must be accounted for in some other way.

In Herman Melville's romance of *Moby Dick, or The White Whale*, there is a long dissertation, perhaps the finest thing in the book, on whiteness in nature, and

SNOW AT EL CARMEN

its effect on the mind. It is an interesting and somewhat obscure subject; and, as Melville is the only writer I know who has dealt with it, and something remains to be said, I may look to be pardoned for dwelling on it at some length in this place.

Melville recalls the fact that in numberless natural objects whiteness enhances beauty, as if it imparted some special virtue of its own, as in marbles, japonicas, pearls; that the quality of whiteness is emblematic of whatever we regard as high and most worthy of reverence; that it has for us innumerable beautiful and kindly associations. "Yet," he goes on to say, "for all these accumulated associations with whatever is sweet, and honourable, and sublime, there lurks an illusive something in the innermost idea of this hue which strikes more of panic to the soul than the redness which affrights in blood." He is no doubt right that there is a mysterious illusive *something* affecting us in the thought of whiteness; but, then, so illusive is it, and in most cases so transient in its effect, that only when we are told of it do we look for and recognize its existence in us. And this only with regard to certain things, a distinction which Melville failed to see, this being his first mistake in his attempt to "solve the incantation of whiteness." His second and greatest error is in the assumption that the quality of whiteness, apart from the object it is associated with, has anything extranatural or supernatural to the mind. There is no "supernaturalism in the hue," no "spectralness over the fancy," in the thought of the whiteness of white clouds; of the white horses of the sea; of white sea-birds, and white water-fowl, such as swans, storks, egrets, ibises, and many others; nor in white beasts, not dangerous to us, wild or domestic, nor in white flowers. These may bloom in such profusion as to whiten whole fields, as with snow, and their whiteness yet be no more to the fancy than the yellows, purples, and reds of other kinds. In the same way the whiteness of the largest masses of white clouds has no more of supernaturalness to the mind than the blueness of the sky and the greenness of vegetation. Again, on still hot days on the pampas the level earth is often seen glittering with the silver whiteness of the mirage; and this is also a common natural appearance to the mind, like the whiteness of summer clouds, of sea foam, and of flowers.

From all these examples, and many others might be added, it seems evident that the "illusive something," which Melville found in the innermost idea of this hue—a something that strikes more of panic to the soul than the redness which affrights in blood—does not reside in the quality of whiteness itself.

After making this initial mistake, he proceeds to name all those natural objects which, being white, produce in us the various sensations he mentions, mysterious and ghostly, and in various ways unpleasant and painful. What is it, he asks, that in the albino so peculiarly repels and shocks the eye, as that sometimes he is loathed by his own kith and kin? He has a great deal to say of the polar bear, and the white shark of the tropical seas, and concludes that it is their whiteness that makes them so much more terrible to us than other savage rapacious creatures that are dangerous to man. He speaks of the muffled rolling of a milky sea; the rustlings of the festooned frost of mountains; the desolate shiftings of the windrowed snows of prairies. Finally, he asks, whence, in peculiar moods, comes that gigantic phantom over the soul at the bare mention of a White Sea, a White Squall, White Mountains, etc., etc.?

He assumes all along that the cause of the feeling, however it may differ in degree and otherwise, according to the nature and magnitude of the subject, is one and the same in all cases, that the cause is in the whiteness, and not in the object with which that quality is associated.

The albino case need not detain us long; and here Melville's seafaring experiences might have suggested a better explanation. Sailors, I am convinced from observation, are very primitive in their impulses, and hate, and often unite in persecuting, a companion who, owing to failing strength or some physical defect, is not able to do his share of the work. Savages and semi-barbarous people often cherish a strong animosity against a constantly ailing, crippled, or otherwise defective member of the community: and albinism is associated with weakness of vision, and other defects, which might be a sufficient cause of the aversion. Even among the highly civilized and humane, the sight of sickness is probably always, in some measure, repulsive and shocking, especially in cases in which the skin loses its natural colour, such as an consumption, chlorosis, and jaundice. This natural and universal cause of dislike of the albino would be strengthened among pure savages by the superstitious element—the belief that the abnormal paleness of the individual was supernatural, that want of colour signified absence of soul.

As to the white shark of the tropics, the simplest explanation of the greater terror inspired by this creature would be that, being white, and therefore conspicuous above all other dangerous creatures, the sight would be more attracted to it, its image would become more fixed, and look larger and more formidable in the mind, and it would be more often thought about apprehensively, with the result that there would be a predisposition to regard it with a fear exceeding that inspired by other creatures equally or even more dangerous to human life, but inconspicuously coloured, hence not so vividly seen, and creating no such distinct and persistent mental image. Let us consider what would be the effect of the appearance of a warrior, habited in snowy white, or shining gold, or vivid scarlet, or flame-colour, among a host of contending men, fighting in the old fashion with sword and spear and battle-axe, all clothed and armoured in dull neutral or sombre colours. Wherever he appeared every eye would be attracted to him; his movements and actions would be followed with intense interest by all, and by his antagonists with keen apprehension; every time he parried a blow aimed at his life he would appear invulnerable to the lookers-on, and whenever an enemy went down before him it would seem that a supernatural energy nerved his arm, that the gods were fighting on his side. So great is the effect of mere conspicuousness! Any white savage beast would, because of its whiteness, or conspicuousness, seem more dangerous than another; and a Chillingham bull, no doubt, inspires more fear in a person exposed to attack than a red or black bull. On the other hand, sheep and lambs, although their washed fleeces look whiter than snow, are regarded as indifferently as rabbits and fawns, and their whiteness is nothing to us.

Something more remains to be said about whiteness in animals, which must come later. It will be more in order to speak first of the whiteness of snow, and the whiteness of a seething ocean. We are all capable of experiencing something of that feeling, so powerfully described by Melville, at the sight of the muffled rollings of a milky sea, and white mountains, and the desolate shiftings of windrowed snows on vast stretches of level earth. But doubtless in many the feeling would be slight; there is an "illusive something" in us when we behold the earth suddenly whitened with snow; but the feeling does not last, and is speedily forgotten, or else set down as an effect of mere novelty. In Melville it was very strong; it stirred him deeply, and caused him to ponder with awe on its meaning; and the conclusion he came to was that it is an instinct in us—an instinct similar to that of the horse with regard to the smell of some animal which has the effect of violently agitating it. He calls it an inherited experience. "Nor, in some things," he says, "does the common hereditary experience of all mankind fail to bear witness to the supernaturalism of this hue." Finally, the feeling speaks to us of appalling things in a remote past of unimaginable desolations, and stupendous calamities overwhelming the race of man.

It is a sublime conception, adequately expressed; and as we read the imagination pictures to us the terrible struggle of our hardy barbarous progenitors against the bitter killing cold of the last glacial period; but the picture is vague, like striving human figures in a landscape half obliterated by wind-driven snow. It was a struggle that endured for long ages, until the gigantic white phantom, from which men sought everywhere to fly, came to be a phantom of the mind, a spectralness over the fancy, and instinctive horror, which the surviving remnant transmitted by inheritance down to our own distant times.

It is more than likely that cold has been one of the oldest and deadliest enemies to our race; nevertheless, I reject Melville's explanation in favour of another, which seems more simple and satisfactory—to its author, at all events: which is, that that mysterious something that moves us at the sight of snow springs from the animism that exists in us, and our animistic way of regarding all exceptional phenomena. The mysterious feelings produced in us by the sight of a snow-whitened earth are not singular, but are similar in character to the feelings caused by many other phenomena, and they may be experienced, although in a very slight degree, almost any day of our lives, if we live with nature.

It must be explained that *animism* is not used here in the sense that Tyler gives it in his *Primitive Culture*: in that work it signifies a theory of life, a philosophy of primitive man, which has been supplanted among civilized people by a more advanced philosophy. Animism here means not a doctrine of souls that survive the bodies and objects they inhabit, but the mind's projection of itself into nature, its attribution of its own sentient life and intelligence to all things—that primitive universal faculty on which the animistic philosophy of the savage is founded. When our philosophers tell us that this faculty is obsolete in us, that it is effectually killed by ratiocination, or that it only survives for a period in our children, I believe they are wrong, a fact which they could find out for themselves if, leaving their books and theories, they would take a solitary walk on a moonlit night in the "Woods of Westermain," or any other woods, since all are enchanted.

Let us remember that our poets, who speak not scientifically but in the language of passion, when they say that the sun rejoices in the sky and laughs at the storm; that the earth is glad with flowers in spring, and the autumn fields happy; that the clouds frown and weep, and the wind sighs and "utters something mournful on its way"—that in all this they speak not in metaphor, as we are taught to say, but that in moments of excitement, when we revert to primitive conditions of mind, the earth and all nature is alive and intelligent, and feels as we feel. When, after a spell of dull weather, the sun unexpectedly shines out warm and brilliant, who has not felt in that first glad instant that all nature shared his conscious gladness? Or, in the first hours of a great bereavement, who has not experienced a feeling of wonder and even resentment at the sight of blue smiling skies and a sun-flushed earth?

"We have all," says Vignoli, "however unaccustomed to give an account of our acts and functions, found ourselves in circumstances which produced the momentary personification of natural objects. The sight of some extraordinary phenomenon produces a vague sense of someone acting with a given purpose." Not assuredly of "someone" outside of and above the natural phenomenon, but in and one with it, just as the act of a man proceeds from him, and is the man.

It is doubtless true that we are animistic to this extent only at rare moments, and in exceptional circumstances, and during certain aspects of nature that recur only at long intervals. And of all such aspects of nature and extraordinary phenomena, snow is perhaps the most impressive, and is certainly one of the most widely known on the earth, and most intimately associated in the mind with the yearly suspension of nature's beneficent activity, and all that this means to the human family—the failure of food and consequent want, and the suffering and danger from intense cold. This traditional knowledge of an inclement period in nature only serves to intensify the animism that finds a given purpose in all natural phenomena, and sees in the whiteness of earth the sign of a great unwelcome change. Change not death, since nature's life is eternal; but its sweet friendly warmth and softness have died out of it; there is no longer any recognition, any bond; and if we were to fall down and perish by the wayside, there would be no compassion: it is sitting apart and solitary, cold and repelling, its breath suspended, in a trance of grief or passion; and although it sees us it is as though it saw us not, even as we see pebbles and withered leaves on the ground, when some great sorrow has dazed us, or when some deadly purpose is in our heart.

Just as with regard to snow the animistic feeling is strongest in those who inhabit regions where winter is severe, and who annually see this change in nature, so the "muffled rollings of a milky sea" will strike more of panic to the sailor's soul than to that of the landsman. Melville relates an anecdote of an old sailor who swooned from terror at the sight of an ocean white with the foam of breakers among which the ship was driven. He afterwards declared that it was not the

A MILKY SEA

thought of the danger, for to danger he was accustomed, but the whiteness of the sea that overcame him. And to his animistic mind that whiteness was nothing but the sign of ocean's wrath—the sight of its tremendous passion and deadly purpose proved too appalling.

There is no doubt that the conditions of the sailor's life tend to bring out and strengthen the latent animism that is in all of us; the very ship he navigates is to his mind alive and intelligent, how much more the ocean, which, even to landsmen on each return to it after an interval, seems no mere expanse of water, but a living conscious thing. It was only my strangeness to the sea which prevented the sight of its whiteness from affecting me profoundly: animism in me is strongest with regard to terrestrial phenomena, with which I am more familiar.

To return, before concluding this chapter, to the subject of white animals. And first a word or two concerning the great polar bear: is it not probable that the extreme fear it inspires, which is said by those who have encountered this animal to exceed greatly that which is experienced at the sight of other savage beasts that are dangerous to man, is due to its association with the death-like repellent whiteness and desolation of polar scenery?

With regard to abnormal whiteness in animals that are familiar to us, the sight always affects us strangely, even in so innocent and insignificant a creature as a starling, or blackbird, or lapwing. The rarity, conspicuousness, and abnormality in colour of the object are scarcely enough to account for the intensity of the interest excited. Among savages the distinguishing whiteness is sometimes regarded as supernatural: and this fact inclines me to believe that, just as any extraordinary phenomenon produces a vague idea of someone acting with a given purpose, so in the case of the white animal, its whiteness has not come by accident and chance, but is the result of the creature's volition and the outward sign of some excellence of the intelligent soul distinguishing it from its fellows. In Patagonia I heard of a case bearing on this point. On the plain some thirty miles east of Salinas Grandes, in a small band of ostriches there appeared one pure white individual. Some of the Indians, when out hunting, attempted its capture, but they soon ceased to chase it, and it was called thereafter the god of the ostriches, and it was said among them that some great disaster, perhaps death, would overtake any person who should do it harm.

IX

IDLE DAYS

BEFORE the snow, which has given rise to so long a digression, had quite ceased falling the blue sky was smiling again, and I set forth on my muddy walk home. Under the brilliant sun the white mantle very soon began to exhibit broad black lines and rents; and in a brief space of time the earth had recovered its wonted appearance—the cheerful greenish-bluish-grey, which is Nature's livery at all times in this part of Patagonia; while from the dripping bushes the birds resumed their singing.

If the birds of this region do not excel those of other lands in sweetness, compass, and variety (and I am not sure, that they do not) for constancy in singing they indubitably carry the palm. In spring and early summer their notes are incessant; and the choir is then led by that incomparable melodist, the white-banded mocking-bird, a summer visitor. Even in the coldest months of winter, June and July, when the sun shines, the hoarse crooning of the spotted *Columba*, resembling that of the wood pigeon of Europe, and the softer, more sigh-like lamentations of the *Zenaida maculata*, so replete with wild pathos, are heard from the leafless willows fringing the river. Meanwhile, in the bosky uplands, one hears the songs of many passerine species; and always amongst them, with lively hurried notes, the black-headed Magellanic siskin. The scarlet-breasted or military starling sings on the coldest days and during the most boisterous weather: nor can the rainiest sky cheat the grey finches, *Diuca minor*, of their morning and evening hymns, sung by many individuals in joyous concert. The common mocking-bird is still more indefatigable, and sheltering himself from the cold blast continues till after dark warbling out snatches of song from his inexhaustible repertory; his own music being apparently necessary as food and air to his existence.

Warm lovely days succeeded the snowfall. Rising each morning I could reverently exclaim with the human singer,

O gift of God! O perfect day!
Whereon should no man work but play.

Days windless and serene to their very end, bright with a cloudless sky, and sunshine sweet and pleasant to behold, making the grey solitudes smile as if conscious of the heavenly influence. It is a common saying in this country that "once in a hundred years, a man dies in Patagonia." I do not think any other region of the globe can boast of a saying to equal that; though it has been ill-naturedly suggested that the proverb might owe its origin to the fact that most people in Patagonia meet with some violent end. I do not myself believe there is any climate in the world to compare with the winter of the east coast of Patagonia; and although its summer might seem disagreeable to some persons on account of the violent winds that prevail at that season, the atmosphere at all times is so dry and pure as to make pulmonary complaints unknown. A wealthy tradesman of the town told me that from boyhood he suffered from weak lungs and asthma; in search of health he left his country, Spain, and settled in Buenos Ayres, where he formed ties and entered into business. But his old enemy found him there; his asthma became worse and worse, and at last, on his doctor's recommendation, he went on a visit to Patagonia, where in a short time he was restored to complete health—such health as he had never previously known. He went back rejoicing to Buenos Ayres, only to fall ill again and to find his life growing a burden to him. Finally, in desperation, he sold his business and went back to the only country where existence was possible; and when I knew him he had been permanently settled there for about fourteen years, during which time he had enjoyed the most perfect health.

But he was not happy. He confided to me that he had purchased health at a very heavy cost, since he found it impossible ever to accommodate himself to such a rude existence; that he was essentially a child of civilization, a man of the pavement, whose pleasure was in society, in newspapers, the play, and in the cafe where one meets one's friends of an evening and has a pleasant game of dominoes. As these things which he valued were merely dust and ashes to me, I did not sympathize deeply with his discontent, nor consider that it mattered much which portion of the globe he made choice of for a residence. But the facts of his case interested me; and if I should have a reader who has other ideals, who has felt the mystery and glory of life overcoming his soul with wonder and desire, and who bears in his system the canker of consumption which threatens to darken the vision prematurely—to such a one I would say, TRY PATAGONIA. It is far to travel, and in place of the smoothness of Madeira there would be roughness; but how far men go, into what rough places, in search of rubies and ingots of gold; and life is more than these.

During this beautiful weather merely to exist has seemed to me a sufficient pleasure: sometimes rowing on the river, which is here about nine hundred feet wide—going up to the town with the tide and returning with the current when only a slight exertion suffices to keep the boat swiftly gliding over the pure green water. At other times I amuse myself by seeking for the resinous gum, known here by its Indian name *maken*. The scraggy wide-spreading bush, a kind of juniper, it is found on, repays me with many a scratch and rent for all the amber tears I steal. The gum is found in little lumps on the under side of the lower branches, and is, when fresh, semi-transparent and sticky as bird-lime. To fit it for use the natives make it into pellets, and hold it on the point of a stick over a basin of cold water; a coal of fire is then approached to it, causing it to melt and trickle down by drops into the basin. The drops, hardened by the process, are then kneaded with the fingers, cold water being added occasionally, till the gum becomes thick and opaque like putty. To chew it properly requires a great deal of practice, and when this indigenous art has been acquired a small ball of maken may be kept in the mouth two or three hours every day, and used for a week or longer without losing its agreeable resinous flavour or diminishing in bulk, so firmly does it hold together. The maken-chewer, on taking the ball or quid from his mouth, washes it and puts it by for future use, just as one does with a tooth-brush. Chewing gum is not merely an idle habit, and the least that can be said in its favour is that it allays the desire for excessive smoking—no small advantage to the idle dwellers, white or red, in this desert land; it also preserves the teeth by keeping them free from extraneous matter, and gives them such a pearly lustre as I have never seen outside of this region.

My own attempts at chewing maken have, so far, proved signal failures. Somehow the gum invariably spreads itself in a thin coat over the interior of my mouth, covering the palate like a sticking-plaster and enclosing the teeth in a stubborn rubber case. Nothing will serve to remove it when it comes to this pass but raw suet, vigorously chewed for half an hour, with occasional sips of cold water to harden the delightful mixture and induce it to come away. The culmination of the mess is when the gum spreads over the lips and becomes entangled in the hairs that overshadow them; and when the closed mouth has to be carefully opened with the fingers, until these also become sticky and hold together firmly as if united by a membrane. All this comes about through the neglect of a simple precaution, and never happens to the accomplished masticator, who is to the manner born. When the gum is still fresh occasionally it loses the quality of stiffness artificially imparted to it, and suddenly, without rhyme or reason, retransforms itself into the raw material as it came from the tree. The adept, knowing by certain indications when this is about to happen, takes a mouthful of cold water at the critical moment, and so averts a result so discouraging to the novice. Maken-chewing is a habit common to everybody throughout the entire territory of Patagonia, and for this reason I have described the delightful practice at some length.

When disinclined for gum-chewing I ramble for hours through the bushes to listen to the birds, learning their language and making myself familiar with their habits. How coy are some species whose instincts ever impel them to concealment! What vigilance, keen and never relaxed, is theirs! Difficult even to catch a passing glimpse of them as they skulk from notice, how much more so to observe them disporting themselves without fear or restraint, unconscious of any intrusive presence! Yet such observation only satisfies the naturalist, and when obtained it amply repays the silence, the watching, and the waiting it costs. In some cases the opportunities are so rare that whilst they are being sought, and without ever actually occurring, the observer day by day grows more familiar with the manners of the wild creatures that still succeed in eluding his sight.

Now the little cock (*Rhinocrypta lanceolata*), an amusing bird that lives on the ground, carries its tail erect and looks wonderfully like a very small bantam, has spied me, and, full of alarm, utters his loud chirrup from an adjacent bush. Gently I steal towards him, careful to tread on the sand, then peer cautiously into the foliage. For a few moments he scolds me with loud, emphatic tones, and then is silent. Fancying him still in the same place, I walk about the bush many times, striving to catch sight of him. Suddenly the loud chirrup is resumed in a bush a stone's-throw away; and soon, getting tired of this game of hide-and-seek, in which the bird has all the fun and I all the seeking, I give it up ramble on.

Then, perhaps, the measured, deep, percussive tones of the subterranean *Ctenomys*, well named *oculto* in the vernacular, resound within a dozen yards

CTENOMYS MAGELLANICA

of my feet. So near and loud do they sound, I am convinced the shy little rodent has ventured for a moment to visit the sunshine. I might possibly even catch a momentary glimpse of him, sitting, trembling at the slightest sound, turning his restless bright black eyes this way and that to make sure that no insidious foe is lurking near. For while the mole's eyes have dwindled to mere specks, a dark subterranean life has had a contrary effect on the *oculto's* orbs, and made them large, although not so large as in some cave-rodents. On tiptoe, scarcely breathing, I approach the intervening bush and peep round it, only to find that he has already vanished! A hillock of damp, fresh sand, bearing the impress of a tail and a pair of little feet, show that he has been busy there, and had sat only a moment ago swelling the silky fur of his bosom with those deep, mysterious sounds. Cautiously, silently, I had approached him, but the subtle fox and the velvet-footed cat would have drawn near with still greater silence and caution, yet he would have baffled them both. Of all shy mammals he is the shyest; in him fear is never overcome by curiosity, and days, even weeks, may now elapse before I come so near seeing the *Ctenomys magellanica* again.

It is near sunset, and, hark! as I ramble on I hear in the low scrub before me the crested tinamous (*Calodromus elegans*), the wild fowl of this region, and in size like the English pheasant, just beginning their evening call. It is a long, sweetly modulated note, somewhat flute-like, and sounding clear and far in the quiet evening air. The covey is a large one, I conjecture, for many voices are joined in the concert. I mark the spot and walk on; but at my approach, however quiet and masked with bushes it may be, one by one the shy vocalists drop their parts. The last to cease repeats his note half a dozen times, then the contagion reaches him and he too becomes silent. I whistle and he answers; for a few minutes we keep up the duet, then, aware of the deception, he is silent again. I resume my walk and pass and repass fifty times through the scattered scrub, knowing all the time that I am walking about amongst the birds, as they sit turning their furtive eyes to watch my movements, yet concealed from me by that wonderful adaptive resemblance in the colour of their plumage to the sear grass and foliage around them, and by that correlated instinct which bids them sit still in their places. I find many evidences of their presence— prettily mottled feathers dropped when they preened their wings, also a dozen or twenty neat circular hollows scooped in the sand in which they recently dusted themselves. There are also little chains of footprints running from one hollow to the other; for these pulverizing pits serve the same birds every day and, there being more birds in the covey than there are pits, the bird that does not quickly secure a place doubtless runs from pit to pit in search of one unoccupied. Doubtless there are many pretty quarrels too; and the older, stronger bird, regular in the observance of this cleanly luxurious habit, must, *per fas et nefas,* find accommodation somewhere.

CALODROMUS ELEGANS

I leave the favoured haunt, but when hardly a hundred yards away the birds resume their call in the precise spot I have just quitted; first one and then two are heard, then twenty voices join in the pleasing concert. Already fear, an emotion strong but transitory in all wild creatures, has passed from them, and they are free and happy as if my wandering shadow had never fallen across them.

Twilight comes and brings an end to these useless researches; useless, I say, and take great delight in saying it, for if there is anything one feels inclined to abhor in this placid land, it is the doctrine that all our investigations into nature are for some benefit, present or future, to the human race.

Night also brings supper, welcome to the hungry man, and hours of basking in the genial light and warmth of a wood fire, I on one side, and my bachelor host on the other. The smoke curls up from our silent lips, whilst idle reveries possess our minds—fit termination of a day spent as we have spent it: for my host is also an idler, only a more accomplished one than I can ever hope to be.

We read little; my companion has never learnt letters, and I, less fortunate in that respect, having only been able to discover one book in the house, a Spanish *Libro de Misa*, beautifully printed in red and black letters, and bound in scarlet morocco. I take this book and read, until he, tired of listening to prayers, however beautiful, challenges me to a game of cards. For some time we could not hit on anything to play for, cigarettes being common property, but at length we thought of stories, the loser of most games during the evening to tell the other a story, as a mild soporific, after retiring. My host invariably won, which was not very strange; for he had been a professional gambler most of his days, and could deal himself the killing cards every time he shuffled. More than once I caught him in the very act, for he despised his antagonist and was careless, and lectured him on the immorality of cheating at cards, even when we were only playing for love, or for something next door to it. My strictures amused his Patagonian mind very much; he explained that what I called cheating was only a superior kind of skill acquired by much study and long practice; so it happened that every night I was compelled to draw on my memory or invention for stories to pay my losses.

Only at night one feels the winter here, but in September one knows that it has gone, though summer birds have not yet returned, nor the forest of dwarf mimosas burst into brilliant yellow bloom. Through all seasons the general aspect of nature remains the same, owing to the grey undeciduous foliage of the tree and shrub vegetation covering the country.

As spring advances each day dawns apparently more brilliantly beautiful than the preceding one, and after breakfast I roam forth, unencumbered with gun, in search of recreation.

Hard by my residence there is a hill called the "Parrots' Cliff," where the swift current of the river, altering its course, has eaten into the shore till a sheer smooth precipice over a hundred feet high has been formed. In ancient times the summit must have been the site of an Indian village, for I am continually picking up arrow-heads here; at present the face of the cliff is inhabited by a flock of screaming Patagonian parrots, that have their ancestral breeding-holes in the soft rock. It is also haunted by a flock of pigeons that have taken to a feral life, by one pair of little hawks (*Falco sparverius*), and a colony of purple martins; only these last have not yet returned from their equatorial wanderings. Quiet reigns along the precipice when I reach it, for the vociferous parrots are away feeding. I lie down on my breast and peer over the edge; far, far beneath me a number of coots are peacefully disporting themselves in the water. I take a stone the bigness of my hand, and, poising it over the perilous rim, drop it upon them: down, down, down it drops; oh, simple, unsuspecting coots, beware! Splash it falls in the middle of the flock, sending up a column of water ten feet high, and then what a panic seizes on the birds! They tumble over as if shot, dive down incontinently, then reappearing, pause not to look about them, but spring away with all that marvellous flutter and splutter of which coots alone are capable; the wings beating rapidly, the long legs and lobed feet sprawling behind or striking the surface, away they scud, flying and tumbling over the water, spreading needless alarm through flocks of pin-tails, shrill-voiced widgeons, and stately black-necked swans, but never pausing until the opposite shore of the river is reached.

Pleased with the success of my experiment, I quit the precipice, to the great relief of the blue pigeons and of the little hawks; these last having viewed my proceedings with great jealousy, for they have already taken possession of a hole in the rock with a view to nidification.

Further on in my rambles I discover a nest of the large black leaf-cutting ant (Œcodoma) found over the entire South American continent—and a leading member of that social tribe of insects of which it has been said that they rank intellectually next to ourselves. Certainly this ant, in its actions, simulates man's intellect very closely, and not in the unpleasant manner of species having warrior castes and slaves. The leaf-cutter is exclusively agricultural in its habits, and constructs subterranean galleries, in which it stores fresh leaves in amazing quantities. The leaves are not eaten, but are cut up into small pieces and arranged in beds: these beds quickly become frosted over with a growth of minute fungus; this the ant industriously gathers and stores for use, and when the artificial bed is exhausted the withered leaves are carried out to make room for a layer of fresh ones. Thus the Œcodoma literally *grows* its own food, and in this respect appears to have reached a stage beyond the most highly developed ant communities hitherto described. Another interesting fact is that, although the leaf-cutters have a peaceful disposition, never showing resentment except when gratuitously interfered with, they are just as courageous as any purely predatory species, only their angry emotions and warlike qualities always appear to be dominated by reason and the public good. Occasionally a community of leaf-cutters goes to war with a neighbouring colony of ants of some other species; in this, as in everything else, they seem to act with a definite purpose and great deliberation. Wars are infrequent, but in all those I have witnessed—and I have known this species from childhood—the fate of the nation is decided in one great pitched battle. A spacious bare level spot of ground is chosen, where the contending armies meet, the fight raging for several hours at a stretch, to be renewed on several consecutive days. The combatants, equally sprinkled over a wide area, are seen engaged in single combat or in small groups, while others, non-fighters, run briskly about removing the dead and disabled warriors from the field of battle.

Perhaps some reader, who has made the acquaintance of nature in a London square, will smile at my wonderful ant story. Well, I have smiled too, and cried a little, perhaps, when, witnessing one of these "decisive battles of the world," I have thought that the stable civilization of the Œcodoma ants will probably continue to flourish on the earth when our feverish dream of progress has ceased to vex it. Does that notion seem very fantastical? Might not such a thought have crossed the mind of some priestly Peruvian, idly watching the labours of a colony of leaf-cutters—a thousand years ago, let us say, before the canker had entered into his system to make it long ere the Spaniard came, ripe for death? History preserves one brief fragment which goes to show that the Incas themselves were not altogether enslaved by the sublime traditions they taught the vulgar; that they also possessed, like philosophic moderns, some conception of that implacable power of nature which orders all things, and is above Viracocha and Pachacamac and the majestic gods that rode the whirlwind and tempest, and had their thrones on the everlasting peaks of the Andes. Five or six centuries have probably made little change in the economy of the *Œcodoma*, but the splendid civilization of the children of the sun, albeit it bore on the face of it the impress of unchangeableness and endless duration, has vanished utterly from the earth.

To return from this digression. The nest I have discovered is more populous than London, and there are several roads diverging from it, each one four or five inches wide, and winding away hundreds of yards through the bushes. Never was any thoroughfare in a great city fuller of busy hurrying people than one of these roads. Sitting beside one, just where it wound over the soft yellow sand, I grew tired of watching the endless procession of little toilers, each one carrying a leaf in his jaws; and very soon there came into my ear a whisper from somebody:

> Who finds some mischief still
> For idle hands to do.

It is always pleasant to have even a hypothetical somebody on whom to shuffle the responsibility of our evil actions. Warning my conscience that I am only going to try a scientific experiment, one not nearly so cruel as many in which the pious Spallanzani took great delight, I scoop a deep pit in the sand; and the ants, keeping on their way with their usual blind, stupid sagacity, tumble pell-mell over each other into it. On, on they come, in scores and in hundreds, like an endless flock of sheep jumping down a pit into which the crazy bell-wether has led the way: soon the hundreds have swelled to thousands, and the yawning gulf begins to fill with an inky mass of wriggling, biting, struggling ants. Every falling leaf-cutter carries down a few grains of treacherous sand with it, making the descent easier, and soon the pit is full to overflowing. In five minutes more they will all be out again at their accustomed labours, just a little sore about the legs, perhaps, where they have bitten one another, but no worse for their tumble, and all that will remain of the dreadful cavern will be a slight depression in the soil.

Satisfied with the result, I resume my solitary ramble, and by-and-by coming upon a fine Escandalosa bush I resolve to add incendiarism to my list of misdeeds. It might appear strange that a bush should be called Escandalosa, which means simply Scandalous, or, to prevent mistakes, which simply means Scandalous; but this is one of those quaint names the Argentine peasants have bestowed on some of their curious plants—dry love, the devil's snuff-box, bashful weed, and many others. The Escandalosa is a wide-spreading shrub, three to five feet high, thickly clothed with prickly leaves, and covered all the year round with large pale-yellow immortal flowers; and the curious thing about the plant is that when touched with fire it blazes up like a pile of wood shavings, and is immediately consumed to ashes with a marvellous noise of hissing and crackling. And thus the bush I have found burns itself up on my placing a lighted match at its roots.

DOLCHOTIS PATAGONICA

I enjoy the spectacle amazingly while it lasts, the brilliant tongues of white flame darting and leaping through the dark foliage making a very pretty show; but presently, contemplating the heap of white ashes at my feet where the green miracle, covered with its everlasting flowers, flourished a moment ago, I began to feel heartily ashamed of myself. For how have I spent my day? I remember with remorse the practical joke perpetrated on the simple-minded coots, also the consternation caused to a whole colony of industrious ants; for the idler looks impatiently on the occupations of others, and is always glad of an opportunity of showing up the futility of their labours. But what motive had I in burning this flowering bush that neither toiled nor spun, this slow-growing plant, useless amongst plants as I amongst my fellow-men? Is it not the fact that something of the spirit of our simian progenitors survives in us still? Who that has noticed monkeys in captivity—their profound inconsequent gravity and insane delight in their own unreasonableness—has not envied them their immunity from cold criticism? That intense relief which all men, whether grave or gay, experience in escaping from conventional trammels into the solitude, what is it, after all, but the delight of going back to nature, to be for a time, what we are always pining to be, wild animals, unconfined monkeys, with nothing to restrain us in our gambols, and with only a keener sense of the ridiculous to distinguish us from other creatures?

But what, I suddenly think, if some person in search of roots and gums, or only curious to know how a field naturalist spends his days, gunless in the woods, should be secretly following and watching me all the time?

I spring up alarmed, and cast my eyes rapidly around me. Merciful heavens! what is that suspiciously human-looking object seventy yards away amongst the bushes? Ah, relief inexpressible, it is only the pretty hare-like *Dolichotis patagonica* sitting up on his haunches, gazing at me with a meek wonder in his large round timid eyes.

The little birds are bolder and come in crowds, peering curiously from every twig, chirping and twittering with occasional explosions of shrill derisive laughter. I feel myself blushing all over my face; their jeering remarks become intolerable, and, owl-like, I fly from then persecutions to hide myself in a close thicket. There, with grey-green curtains about and around me, I lie on a floor of soft yellow sand, silent and motionless as my neighbour the little spider seated on his geometric web, till the waning light and the flute of the tinamou send me home to supper.

X

BIRD MUSIC IN SOUTH AMERICA

SUMMER, winter and spring, it was an unfailing pleasure in Patagonia to listen to the singing of the birds. They were most abundant where the cultivated valley with its groves and orchards was narrowest, and the thorny wilderness of the upland close at hand; just as in England small birds abound most where plantations of fruit trees exist side by side with or near to extensive woods and commons. In the first there is an unfailing supply of insect food, the second affords them the wild cover they prefer, and they pass frequently from one to the other. At a distance from the river birds were not nearly so abundant, and in the higher uplands a hundred miles from the coast they were very scarce.

When the idle fit was on me it was my custom to ramble in the bushy lands away from the river, especially during the warm spring weather, when there were some fresh voices to be heard of migrants newly arrived from the tropics, and the songs of the resident species had acquired a greater vigour and beauty. It was a pleasure simply to wander on and on for hours, moving cautiously among the bushes, pausing at intervals to listen to some new note; or to hide myself and sit or lie motionless in the middle of a thicket, until the birds forgot or ceased to be troubled at my presence. The common resident mocking-bird was always present, each bird sitting motionless on the topmost spray of his favourite thorn, at intervals emitting a few notes, a phrase, then listening to the others.

But there was one bitter drop in my sweet cup. It vexed my mind and made me almost unhappy to think that travellers and naturalists from Europe, whose works were known to me, were either silent or else said very little (and that mostly depreciatory) of the bird music that was so much to me. Darwin's few words were especially remembered and rankled most in my mind, because he was the greatest and had given a good deal of attention to bird life in southern South America. The highest praise that he gave to a Patagonian songster was that it had "two or three

CALANDRIA MOCKING-BIRD

pleasant notes;" and of the Calandria mocking-bird, one of the finest melodists in La Plata, he wrote that it was nearly the only bird he had seen in South America that regularly took its stand for the purpose of singing; that it was remarkable for possessing a song superior to that of any other kind, and *that its song resembled that of the sedge warbler!*

Speaking of British species, I do not think it could be rightly said that the song of the sedge warbler resembles that of the song-thrush. I do think that the thrush's song often resembles that of the mocking-bird referred to, also that it would scarcely be an exaggeration to say that all the music of the song-thrush might be taken out of the Calandria mocking-bird's performance and not be very greatly missed.

The desire to say something on this subject was strong in me at that time, for, leaving aside the larger question of the bird music of South America, I could not help thinking that these observers had missed the chief excellence of the songsters known to me. But I had no title to speak; I had not heard the nightingale, song-thrush, blackbird, skylark, and all the other members of that famous choir whose melody has been a delight to our race for so many ages; I was without the standard which others had, and being without it, could not be absolutely sure that a mistake had been made, and that the opinion I had formed of the melodists of my own district was not too high. Now that I am familiar with the music of British song-birds in a state of nature the case is different, and I can express myself on the subject without fear and without doubt. But I have no intention of speaking in this place of the South American bird music I know, comparing it with that of England. And this for two reasons. One is that I have already written on this subject in *Argentine Ornithology* and *The Naturalist in La Plata*. The second reason is because bird music, and, indeed, bird sounds generally, are seldom describable. We have no symbols to represent such sounds on paper, hence we are as powerless to convey to another the impression they make on us as we are to describe the odours of flowers. It is hard, perhaps, to convince ourselves of this powerlessness; in my case the saddening knowledge was forced on me in such a way that escape was impossible. No person at a distance from England could have striven harder than I did, by inquiring of those who knew and by reading ornithological works, to get a just idea of the songs of British birds. Yet all my pains were wasted, as I found out afterwards when I heard them, and when almost every song came to me as a surprise. It could not have been otherwise. To name only half a dozen of the lesser British melodists: the little jets of brilliant melody spurted out by the robin; the more sustained lyric of the wren, sharp, yet delicate; the careless half-song half-recitative of the common warbler; the small fragments of dreamy aerial music emitted by the wood wren amidst the high translucent foliage; the hurried, fantastic medley of liquid and grating sounds of the reed warbler; the song, called by some a twitter, of the swallow, in which the quick, upleaping notes seem to dance in the air, to fall more than one at a time on the sense, as if more than one bird sang, spontaneous and glad as the laughter of some fairy-like, unimaginable child— who can give any idea of such sounds as these with such symbols as words! It is easy to say that a song is long or short, varied or monotonous, that a note is sweet, clear, mellow, strong, weak, loud, shrill, sharp, and so on; but from all this we get no idea of the distinctive character of the sound, since these words describe only class, or generic qualities, not the specific and individual. It sometimes seems to help us, in describing a song, to give its feeling, when it strikes us as possessing some human feeling, and call it joyous, glad, plaintive, tender, and so on; but this is, after all, a rough expedient, and, often as not, misleads. Thus, in the case of nightingale, I had been led by reading to expect to hear a distinctly plaintive song, and found it so far from plaintive that I was swayed to the opposite extreme, and pronounced it (with Coleridge) a glad song. But by-and-by I dismissed this notion as equally false with the other; the more I listened the more I admired the purity of sound in some notes, the exquisite phrasing, the beautiful contrasts; the art was perfect, but there was no passion in it all—no *human* feeling. Feeling of some un-human kind there perhaps was, but not gladness, such as we imagine in the skylark's song, and certainly not sorrow, nor anything sad. Again, when we listen to a song that all have agreed to call "tender," we perhaps recognize some quality that faintly resembles, or affects us like, the quality of tenderness in human speech or vocal music; but if we think for a moment, we are convinced that it is not tenderness, that the effect is not quite the same; that we have so described it only because we have no suitable word; that there is really no suggestion of human feeling in it.

The old method of *spelling* bird notes and sounds still finds favour with some easy-going naturalists, and it is possible that those who use it do actually believe that the printed word represents some avian sound to the reader, and that those who have never heard the sound can by this simple means get an idea of it; just as certain arbitrary marks or signs on a sheet of written music represent human sounds. It is fancy and a delusion. We have not yet invented any system of arbitrary signs to represent bird sounds, nor are we likely to invent such a system, because, in the first place, we do not properly know the sounds, and, owing to their number and character, cannot properly know more than a very few of them; and, in the second place, because they are different in each species: and just as our human notation represents solely our human specific sounds, so a notation of one bird's language, that of the skylark, let us say, would not apply to the language of another species, the nightingale, say, on account of the difference in quality and *timbre* of the two.

One cause of the extreme difficulty of describing bird sounds so as to give anything approaching to a correct idea of them, lies in the fact that in most of them, from the loudest—the clanging scream or call that may be heard a distance of two or three miles—to the faintest tinkling or lisping note that might be emitted by a creature no bigger than a fly, there is a certain aerial quality which makes them differ from all other sounds. Doubtless several causes contribute to give them this character. There is the great development of the vocal organ, which makes the voice, albeit finer, more far-reaching than that of other creatures of equal size or larger. The body in birds is less solid; it is filled with air in the bones and feathers, and acts differently as a sounding board; furthermore, the extremely distensible œsophagus, although it has no connection with the trachea, is puffed out with swallowed air when the bird emits its notes, and this air, both when retained and when released, in some way affects the voice. Then, again, the bird sings or calls, as a rule, from a greater elevation, and does not sit squat, like a toad, on his perch, but being lifted above it on his slender legs, the sounds he emits acquire a greater resonance.

There are bird sounds which may be, and often are, likened to other sounds; to bells, to the clanging produced by blows on an anvil, and to various other metallic noises; and to strokes on tightly-drawn metal strings; also to the more or less musical sounds we are able to draw from wood and bone, and from vessels of glass by striking them or drawing the moistened finger-tips along their rims. There are also sounds resembling those that are uttered by mammalians, as bellowings, lowings, bleatings, neighings, barkings, and yelpings. Others simulate the sounds of various musical instruments, and human vocal sounds, as of talking, humming a tune, whistling, laughing, moaning, sneezing, coughing, and so on. But in all these, or in a very large majority, there is an airy resonant quality which tells you, even in a deep wood, in the midst of an unfamiliar fauna, that the new and strange sound is uttered by a bird. The clanging anvil is in the clouds; the tinkling bell is somewhere in the air, suspended on nothing; the invisible human creatures that whistle, and hum airs, and whisper to one another, and clap their hands and laugh, are not bound, like ourselves, to earth, but float hither and thither as they list.

Something of this aerial character is acquired by other sounds, even by the most terrestrial, when heard at a distance in a quiet atmosphere. And some of our finer sounds, as those of the flute and bugle and flageolet, and some others, when heard faintly in the open air, have the airy character of bird notes; with this difference, that they are dim and indistinct to the sense, while the bird's note, although so airy, is of all sounds the most distinct.

Mr. John Burroughes, in his excellent *Impressions of some British Song Birds*, has said, that many of the American songsters are shy wood-birds, seldom seen or heard near the habitations of man, while nearly all the British birds are semi-domesticated, and sing in gardens and orchards; that this fact, in connection with their more soft and plaintive voices, made American song birds seem less to the European traveller than his own. This statement would hold good, and even gain in force, if for North America we should substitute the hot or larger part of South America, or of the Neotropical region, which comprises the whole of America south of the Isthmus of Tehuantepec. Throughout the tropical and subtropical portions of this region, which is vastly richer in species than the northern half of the continent, the songsters certainly do not, like those of Europe, mass themselves about the habitations of men, as if sweet voices were given to them solely for the delectation of human listeners: they are pre-eminently birds of the wild forest, marsh, and savannah, and if one of their chief merits has been overlooked, it is because the European naturalist and collector, whose object is to obtain many specimens, and some new forms, has no time to make himself acquainted with the life habits and faculties of the species he meets with. Again, bird life is extremely scarce in some places within the tropics, and in the deep forest it is often wholly absent. Of British Guiana, Mr. im Thurn writes, "The almost entire absence of sweet bird-notes at once strikes the traveller who comes from thrush and warbler-haunted temperate lands." And Bates says of the Amazonian forests: "The few sounds of birds are of that pensive and mysterious character which intensifies the feeling of solitude rather than imparts a sense of life and cheerfulness."

It is not only this paucity of bird life in large tracts of country which has made the tropics seem to the European imagination a region "where birds forget to sing," and has caused many travellers and naturalists to express so poor an opinion of South American bird music. There remains in most minds something of that ancient notion that brilliant plumaged birds emit only harsh disagreeable sounds—the macaw and the peacock are examples; while the sober-coloured birds of temperate regions, especially of Europe, have the gift of melody; that sweet notes are heard in England, and piercing cries and grating screams within the tropics. As a fact the dull-plumaged species in the hot regions greatly outnumber those that are gaily-coloured. To mention only two South American passerine families, the woodhewers and ant-birds, numbering together nearly five hundred species, or as many as all the species of birds in Europe, are with scarcely an exception sober-coloured. The melodious gold finch, yellow bunting, linnet, blue tit, chaffinch, and yellow wagtail, would look very gay and conspicuous among them. Yet these sober-coloured tropical birds I have mentioned are not singers.

It must also be borne in mind that South America embraces a great variety of climates; that all the vast region, which comprises Chili, the southern half of Argentina, and Patagonia, is in the temperate zone. Also, that a large proportion of the South American songsters belong to families that are universal, in which all the finest voices of Europe are included—thrushes, warblers, wrens, larks, finches. The true thrushes are well represented, and some differ but slightly from European forms—the whistle of the Argentine blackbird is some times mistaken by Englishmen for that of the smaller home bird. The mocking-birds form a group of the same family (Turdidæ) but with more highly-developed vocal powers. It is true that the tanagers, numbering about four hundred species, mostly brilliantly-coloured, some rivalling the humming-birds in the vivid tints and metallic lustre of their plumage, form an exclusively Neotropical family; but they are closely related to the finches, and in the genera in which these two great and melodious families touch and mingle, it is impossible to say of many species which are finches and which tanagers. Another purely American family, with a hundred and thirty known species, a large majority adorned with rich or brilliant or gay and strongly-contrasted colours, are the troupials—Icteridæ and these are closely related to the starlings of the Old World.

Finally, it may be added that the true melodists of the Neotropical region—the passerine birds of the sub-order Oscines, which have the developed vocal organ—number about twelve hundred species:—a big fact when it is remembered that of the five hundred species of birds in Europe, only two hundred and five at the most are classed as songsters, inclusive of fly-catchers, corvine birds and many others which have no melody.

It is clear then, from these facts and figures, that South America is not wanting in songsters, that, on the contrary, it surpasses all other regions of the globe of equal extent in number of species.

It only remains to say something on another matter—namely, the character and value of the music. And here the reader might think that I have got myself into a quandary, since I began by complaining of the unworthy opinion expressed by European writers of the melodists of my country, and at the same time disclaimed any intention of attempting to describe their melody myself, comparing it with that of England. Fortunately for my purpose, not all the travellers in South America, whose words carry weight, have turned a deaf or unappreciative ear to the bird music of the great bird continent: there are notable exceptions; from these I shall proceed to quote a few passages in support of my contention, beginning with Felix de Azara, a contemporary of Buffon, and concluding with the two most illustrious travellers of our own day who have visited South America— Wallace and Bates.

Of Darwin it need only be added that his words on the subject of the songs of birds are so few and of so little value that it is probable that this kind of natural melody gave him little or no pleasure. It is not unusual to meet with those who are absolutely indifferent to it, just as there are others who are not pleasurably moved by human music, vocal or instrumental.

In Spain Azara had been familiar from childhood with the songsters of Europe, and in Paraguay and La Plata he paid great attention to the language of the species he describes. In his ever fresh *Apuntamiento*s he says, "They are mistaken who think there are not as many and as good songsters here as in Europe"; and in the introduction to the same work, referring to Buffon's opinion concerning the inferiority of the American songsters, he writes: "But if a choir of singers were selected in the Old World, and compared with one of equal number gathered in Paraguay, I am not sure which would win the victory." Of the house-wren of La Plata (*Troglodytes furvus*), Azara says that its song is "in style comparable to that of the nightingale, although its phrases are not so delicate and expressive; nevertheless I count it among the first singers." This opinion (with Daines Barrington's misleading table in my mind) made me doubt the correctness of his judgment, or memory, the wren in question being an exceedingly cheerful singer; but when I came to hear the nightingale, about whose song I had formed so false an idea, it seemed to me that Azara was not far out. Nothing here surprised me more than the song of the British wren—a current of sharp high unshaded notes, so utterly different to the brilliant joyous and varied lyric of his near relation in that distant land.

The melodious wren family counts many genera, rich in species, throughout the Neotropical region: and just as in that continent the thrushes have developed a more varied and beautiful music in the mocking-birds, so it has been with this family in such genera as *Thyothorus* and *Cyphorhinus*, which include the celebrated flute-birds and organ-birds of tropical South America. D'Orbigny, in the *Voyage dans l'Amérique Méridionale*, speaks rapturously of one of these wrens, perched on a bough overhanging the torrent, where its rich melodious voice seemed in strange contrast to the melancholy aspect of its surroundings. Its voice, he says, which is

CYPHORHINUS CANTANS

not comparable to anything we have in Europe, exceeds that of the nightingale in volume and expression. Frequently it sounds like a melody rendered by a flute at a great distance; at other times its sweet and varied cadences are mingled with clear piercing tones and deep throat-notes. We have really no words, he concludes, adequate to express the effects of this song, heard in the midst of a nature so redundant, and of mountain scenery so wild and savage.

Mr. Simson, in his *Travels in the Wilds of Ecuador*, writes quite as enthusiastically of a species of *Cyphorhinus* common in that country. It was the mellowest, most beautiful bird music he had ever heard; the song was not quite the same in all individuals, and in tone resembled the most sweet-sounding flute; the musical correctness of the notes was astonishing, and made one imagine the sounds to be produced by human agency.

Even more valuable is the testimony of Bates, one of the least impressible of the savants who have resided in tropical South America; yet his account of the bird is not less fascinating than that of D'Orbigny. "I frequently heard," he writes, "in the neighbourhood of these huts the realejo, or organ-bird (*Cyphorhinus cantans*), the most remarkable songster by far of the Amazonian forest. When its singular notes strike the ear for the first time the impression cannot be resisted that they are produced by a human voice. Some musical boy must be gathering fruits in the thicket, and is singing a few notes to cheer himself. The tones become more fluty and plaintive; they are now those of a flageolet, and notwithstanding the utter impossibility of the thing, one is for a moment convinced that someone is playing that instrument... It is the only songster which makes an impression on the natives, who sometimes rest their paddles whilst travelling in their small canoes, along the shady by-paths, as if struck by the mysterious sound." The sound must be wonderful indeed to produce such an effect!

To finish with quotations, the following sensible passage from Wallace's *Amazon and Rio Negro* should help us greatly in getting rid of an ancient error: "We are inclined to think that the general statement, that the birds of the tropics have a deficiency of song proportionate to their brilliancy of plumage, requires to be modified. Many of the brilliant birds of the tropics belong to families or groups which have no song; but our most brilliantly coloured birds, as the goldfinch and canary, are not less musical, and there are many beautiful little birds here which are equally so. We heard notes resembling those of the blackbird and robin, and one bird gave forth three or four sweet plaintive notes that particularly attracted our attention; while many have peculiar cries, in which words may be traced by the fanciful, and which in the stillness of the forest have a very pleasing effect."

To return, before concluding, to Azara's remark about a choir of birds selected in Paraguay. It seems to me that when the best singers of any two districts have been compared and a verdict arrived at, something more remains to be said. The dulcet strains of a few of the most highly-esteemed songsters contribute only a part, by no means the largest part, of the pleasure we receive from the bird sounds of any district. All natural sounds produce agreeable sensations in the healthy: the patter of rain on the forest leaves, the murmur of the wind, the lowing of kine, the dash of waves on the beach; and so, coming to birds, the piercing tones of the sandpiper, and wail of the curlew; the cries of passing migrants; the cawing of rooks in the elms, and hooting of owls, and the startling scream of the jay in the wood, give us pleasure, scarcely less than that produced by the set song of any melodist. There is a charm in the infinite variety of bird sounds heard in the forests and marshes of southern South America, where birds are perhaps most abundant, exceeding that of many monotonously melodious voices; the listener would not willingly lose any of the indescribable sounds emitted by the smaller species, nor the screams and human-like calls, or solemn deep boomings and drummings of the larger kinds, or even the piercing shrieks which may be heard miles away. Those tremendous voices, that never break the quiet and almost silence of an English woodland, affect us like the sight of mountains, and torrents, and the sound of thunder and of billows breaking on the shore; we are amazed at the boundless energy and overflowing joy of wild bird life. The bird-language of an English wood or orchard, made up in most part of melodious tones, may be compared to a band composed entirely of small wind instruments with a limited range of sound, and which produces no storms of noise, eccentric flights, and violent contrasts, nor anything to startle the listener—a sweet but somewhat tame performance. The South American forest has more the character of an orchestra, in which a countless number of varied instruments take part in a performance in which there are many noisy discords, while the tender spiritual tones heard at intervals seem, by contrast, infinitely sweet and precious.

XI

SIGHT IN SAVAGES

IN Patagonia I added something to my small stock of private facts concerning eyes—their appearance, colour, and expression—and vision, subjects which have had a mild attraction for me as long as I can remember. When, as a boy, I mixed with the gauchos of the pampas, there was one among them who greatly awed me by his appearance and character. He was distinguished among his fellows by his tallness, the thickness of his eyebrows and the great length of his crow-black beard, the form and length of his *facon*, or knife, which was nothing but a sword worn knife-wise, and the ballads he composed, in which were recounted, in a harsh tuneless voice to the strum-strum of a guitar, the hand-to-hand combats he had had with others of his class—fighters and desperadoes—and in which he had always been the victor, for his adversaries had all been slain to a man. But his eyes, his most wonderful feature, impressed me more than anything else; for one was black and the other dark blue. All other strange and extranatural things in nature, of which I had personal knowledge, as, for instance, mushrooms growing in rings, and the shrinking of the sensitive plant when touched, and will-o'-the-wisps and crowing hens, and the murderous attack of social birds and beasts on one of their fellows, seemed less strange and wonderful than the fact that this man's eyes did not correspond, but were the eyes of two men, as if there had been two natures and souls in one body. My astonishment was, perhaps, not unaccountable, when we reflect that the eye is to us the window of the mind or soul, that it expresses the soul, and is, as it were, the soul itself materialized. Some person lately published in England a book entitled, *Soul-Shapes*, treating not only of the shapes of souls but also of their colour. The letter press of this work interests me less than the coloured plates adorning it. Passing over the mixed and vari-coloured souls, which resemble, in the illustrations, coloured maps in an atlas, we come to the blue soul, for which the author has a very special regard. Its blue is like that of the commonest type of blue eye. This curious fancy of a blue soul probably originated in the close association of eye and soul in the mind. It is worthy of note that while the mixed and other coloured souls seem very much out of shape, like an old felt hat or a stranded jelly fish, the pure-coloured blue soul is round, like an iris, and only wanted a pupil to be made an eye.

But the subject of the colour and expression of eyes in man and animals must be reserved for the next chapter; in the present chapter I shall confine myself to the subject of vision in savage and semi-barbarous men as compared with ours.

Here again I recall an incident of my boyhood, and am not sure that it was not this that first gave me an interest in the subject.

One summer day at home, I was attentively listening, out of doors, to a conversation between two men, both past middle life and about the same age, one an educated Englishman, wearing spectacles, the other a native, who was very impressive in his manner, and was holding forth in a loud authoritative voice on a variety of subjects. All at once he fixed his eyes on the spectacles worn by the other, and, bursting into a laugh, cried out, "Why do you always wear those eye-hiding glasses straddled across your nose? Are they supposed to make a man look handsomer or wiser than his fellows, or do you, a sensible person, really believe that you can see better than another man because of them? If so, then all I can say is that it is a fable, a delusion; no man can believe such a thing."

He was only expressing the feeling that all persons of his class, whose lives are passed in the semi-barbarous conditions of the gauchos on the pampas, experience at the sight of such artificial helps to vision as spectacles. They look through a pane of common glass, and it makes the view no clearer, but rather dimmer—how can the two diminutive circular panes carried before the eyes produce any other effect? Besides, their sight as a rule is good when they are young, and as they progress in life they are not conscious of decadence in it; from infancy to old age the world looks, they imagine, the same, the grass as green, the sky as blue as ever, and the scarlet verbenas in the grass just as scarlet. The man lives in his sight; it is his life; he speaks of the loss of it as a calamity great as loss of reason. To see spectacles amuses and irritates him at the same time; he has the monkey's impulse to snatch the idle things from his fellow's nose; for not only is it useless to the wearer, and a sham, but it is annoying to others, who do not like to look at a man and not properly see his eyes, and the thought that is in them.

To the mocking speech he had made the other good-humouredly replied that he had worn glasses for twenty years, that not only did they enable him to see much better than he could without them, but they had preserved his sight from further decadence. Not satisfied with defending himself against the charge of being a fantastical person for wearing glasses, he in his turn attacked the mocker. "How do you know," he said, "that your own eyesight has not degenerated with time? You can only ascertain that by trying on a number of glasses suited to a variety of sights, all in some degree defective. A score of men with decaying sight may be together, and in no two will the sight be the same. You must try on spectacles, as you try on boots, until you find a pair to fit you. You may try mine if you like; our years are the same, and it is just possible that our eyes may be in the same condition."

The gaucho laughed a loud and scornful laugh, and exclaimed that the idea was too ridiculous. "What, see better with this thing!" and he took them gingerly in his hand, and held them up to examine them, and finally put them on his nose— something in the spirit of the person who takes a newspaper twisted into the shape of an extinguisher, and puts it on his head. He looked at the other, then at me then stared all round him, with an expression of utter astonishment, and in the end burst out in loud exclamations of delight. For, strange to say, the glasses exactly suited his vision, which, unknown to him, had probably been decaying for years. "Angels of heaven what is this I see!" he shouted. "What makes the trees look so green—they were never so green before! And so distinct—I can count their leaves! And the cart over there—why, it is red as blood!" And to satisfy himself that it had not just been freshly painted he ran over to it and placed his hand on the wood. It proved hard to convince him that objects had once looked as distinct, and leaves as green, and the sky as blue, and red paint as red, to his natural sight, as they did through those magical glasses. The distinctness and brightness seemed artificial and uncanny. But in he end he was convinced, and then he wanted to keep the spectacles, and pulled out his money to pay for them there and then, and was very much put out when their owner insisted on having them back. However, shortly afterwards a pair was got for him; and with these on his nose he galloped about

GAUCHO WITH SPECTACLES

the country, exhibiting them to all his neighbours, and boasting of the miraculous power they imparted to his eyes of seeing the world as no one else could see it.

My Patagonian host and friend, whose intimate knowledge of cards I have mentioned in a former chapter, once informed me that always after the first few rounds of a game he knew some of the cards, and could recognize them as they were being dealt out, by means of certain slight shades of difference in the colouring of the backs. He had turned his attention to this business when very young, and as he was close upon fifty when he imparted this interesting piece of information, and had always existed comfortably on his winnings, I saw no reason to disbelieve what he told me. Yet this very man, whose vision was keen enough to detect differences in cards so slight that another could not see them, even when pointed out—this preternaturally sharp-eyed individual was greatly surprised when I explained to him that half-a-dozen birds of the sparrow kind, that fed in his courtyard, and sang and built their nests in his garden and vineyard and fields, were not one but six distinct species. He had never seen any difference in them: they all had the same customs, the same motions; in size, colour, and shape they were all one; to his hearing they all chirped and twittered alike, and warbled the same song.

And as it was with this man, so, to some extent, it is with all of us. That special thing which interests us, and in which we find our profit or pleasure, we see very distinctly, and our memories are singularly tenacious of its image; while other things, in which we take only a general interest, or which are nothing to us, are not seen so sharply, and soon become blurred in memory; and if there happens to be a pretty close resemblance in several of them, as in the case of my gambling friend's half-a-dozen sparrows, which, like snowflakes, were "seen rather than distinguished," this indistinctness of their images on the eye and the mind causes them all to appear alike. We have, as it were, two visions—one to which all objects appear vividly and close to us, and are permanently photographed on the mind; the other which sees things at a distance, and with that indistinctness of outline and uniformity of colour which distance gives.

In this place I had proposed to draw on my La Plata note-books for some amusing illustrations of this fact of our two sights; but it is not necessary to go so far afield for illustrations, or to insist on a thing so familiar. "The shepherd knows his sheep," is a saying just as true of this country—of Scotland, at all events—as of the far East. Detectives, also military men who take an interest in their profession, see faces more sharply than most people, and remember them as distinctly as others remember the faces of a very limited number of individuals—of those they love or fear or constantly associate with. Sailors see atmospheric changes which are not apparent to others; and, in like manner, the physician detects the signs of malady in faces which to the uninstructed vision seem healthy enough. And so on through the whole range of professions and pursuits which men have; each person inhabits a little world of his own, as it were, which to others is only part of the distant general blueness obscuring all things, but in which, to him, every object stands out with wonderful clearness, and plainly tells its story.

All this may sound very trite, very trivial, and matter of common knowledge— so common as to be known to every schoolboy, and to the boy that goeth not to school; yet it is because this simple familiar fact has been ignored, or has not always been borne in mind by our masters, that they have taught us an error, namely, that savages are our superiors in visual power, and that the difference is so great that ours is a dim decaying sense compared with their brilliant faculty, and that only when we survey the prospect through powerful field-glasses do we rise to their level, and see the world as they see it. The truth is that the savage sight is no better than ours, although it might seem natural enough to think the contrary, on account of their simple natural life in the desert, which is always green and restful to the eye, or supposed to be so; and because they have no gas nor even candlelight to irritate the visual nerve, and do themselves no injury by poring over miserable books.

Possibly, then, the beginning of the error was in this preconceived notion, that greenness and the absence of artificial light, with other conditions of a primitive life, keep the sight from deteriorating. The eye's adaptiveness did not get sufficient credit. We know how the muscles may be developed by training, that the blacksmith and prizefighter have mightier arms than others; but it was perhaps assumed that the complex structure and extreme delicacy of the eye would make it less adaptive than other and coarser organs. Whatever the origin of the error may have been, it is certain that it has received the approval of scientists, and that they never open their lips on the subject except to give it fresh confirmation. Their researches have brought to light a great variety of eye-troubles, which, in many cases, are not troublesome at all, until they are discovered, named with a startling name, and described in terms very alarming to persons of timid character. Frequently they are not maladies, but inherited defects, like bandy legs, prominent teeth, crushed toes, tender skin, and numberless other malformations. That such eye-defects are as common among savages as among ourselves, I do not say, and to this matter I shall return later on; but until the eyes of savages are scientifically examined, it seems a very bold thing to say that defective colour-sense is due to the inimical conditions of our civilization; for we know as little about the colour-sense of savages as we do about the colour-sense of the old Greeks. That the savage sight is vastly more powerful than ours was perhaps not so bold a thing to say, seeing that in this matter our teachers were misled by travellers' tales, and perhaps by other considerations, as, for instance, the absence of artificial aids to sight among the children of nature. The redskin may be very old, but as he sits sunning himself before his wigwam in the early morning he is never observed to trombone his newspaper.

The reader may spare himself the trouble of smiling, for this is not mere supposition; in this case observation came first and reflection afterwards, for

I happen to know something of savages from experience, and when they were using their eyes in their way, and for their purposes, I used mine for my purpose, which was different. It is true that the redskin will point you out an object in the distance and tell its character, and it will be to your sight only a dark-coloured object, which might be a bush, or stone, or animal of some large kind, or even a house. The secret of the difference is that his eye is trained and accustomed to see certain things, which he looks for and expects to find. Put him where the conditions are new to him and he will be at fault; or, even on his native heath, set him before an unfamiliar or unexpected object, and he will show no superiority over his civilized brother. I have witnessed one instance in which not one but five men were all in fault, and made a wrong guess; while the one person of our party who guessed correctly, or saw better perhaps, was a child of civilization and a reader of books, and, what is perhaps even more, the descendant of a long line of bookish men. This amazed me at the moment, for until then my childlike faith in the belief of Humboldt, and of the world generally, on the subject had never been disturbed. Now I see how this curious thing happened. The object was at such a distance that to all of us alike it presented no definite form, but was merely something dark, standing against a hoary background of tall grass-plumes. Our guides, principally regarding its size, at once guessed it to be an animal which they no doubt expected to find in that place—namely, a wild horse. The other, who did not have that training of the eye and mind for distant objects in the desert which is like an instinct, and, like instinct, is liable to mistakes, and who carefully studied its appearance for himself, pronounced it to be a dark bush. When we got near it turned out to be a clump of tall bulrushes, growing in a place where they had no business to grow, and burnt by drought and frosts to so dark a brown that at a distance they seemed quite black.

In the following case the savage was right. I pointed out an object, dark, far off, so low down as to be just visible above the tall grasses, passing with a falling and rising motion like that of a horseman going at a swinging gallop. "There goes a mounted man," I remarked. "No—a trarú," returned my companion, after one swift glance; the trarú being a large, black, eagle-like bird of the plains, the carancho of the whites—*Polyborus tharus*. But the object was not necessarily more distinct to him than to me; he could not see wings and beak at that distance; but the trarú was a familiar object, which he was accustomed to see at all distances—a figure in the landscape which he looked for and expected to find. It was only a dark blot an the horizon; but he knew the animal's habits and appearance, and that when seen far off, in its low down, dilatory, rising and falling flight, it simulates the appearance of a horseman in full gallop. To know this and a few other things was his vocation. If one had set him to find a reversed little 's' in the middle of a closely-printed page the tears would have run down his brown cheeks, and he would have abandoned the vain quest with aching eyeballs. Yet the proof-reader can find the reversed little 's' in a few moments, without straining his sight.

But it is infinitely more important to the savage of the plains than to us to see distant moving objects quickly and guess their nature correctly. His daily food, the recovery of his lost animals, and his personal safety depend on it; and it is not, therefore, strange that every blot of dark colour, every moving and motionless object on the horizon, tells its story better to him than to a stranger; especially when we consider how small a variety of objects he is called on to see and judge of in the level monotonous region he inhabits.

This quick judging of dimly-seen distant things, the eye- and mind-achievement of the mounted barbarian on the unobstructed plains, is not nearly so admirable as that of his fellow-savage in sub-tropical regions overspread with dense vegetation, with animal life in great abundance and variety, and where half the attention must be given to species dangerous to man, often very small in size. In some hot humid forest districts, the European who should attempt to hunt or explore with bare feet and legs would be pricked and lacerated at almost every step of his progress, and probably get bitten by a serpent before the day's end. Yet the Indian passes his life there, and, naked or half naked, explores the unknown wilderness of thorns, and has only his arrows to provide food for himself and his wife and children. He does not get pierced with thorns and bitten by serpents, because his eye is nicely trained to pick them out in time to save himself. He walks rapidly, but he knows every shade of green, every smooth and crinkled leaf, in that dense tangle, full of snares and deceptions, through which he is obliged to walk; much as leaf resembles leaf, he sets his foot where he can safely set it, or, quickly choosing between two evils, where the prickles and thorns are softest, or, for some reason known to him, hurt least. In like manner he distinguishes the coiled venomous snake, although it lies so motionless—a habit common to the most deadly kinds—and in its dull imitative colouring is so difficult to be distinguished on the brown earth, and among grey sticks and sere and variegated leaves.

A friend of mine, Fontana of Buenos Ayres, who has a life-long acquaintance with the Argentine Indians, expresses the opinion that at the age of twelve years the savage of the Pampas has completed his education, and is thereafter able to take care of himself; but that the savage of the Gran Chaco—the sub-tropical Argentine territory bordering on Paraguay and Bolivia—if left to shift for himself at that age would speedily perish, since he is then only in the middle of his long, difficult, and painful apprenticeship. It was curious and pitiful, he says, to see the little Indian children in the Chaco, when their skins were yet tender, stealing away from their mother, and trying to follow the larger ones playing at a distance. At every step they would fall, and get pricked with thorns or cut with sharp-edged rushes, and tangled in the creepers, and hurt and crying they would struggle on, and in this painful manner learn at last where to set their feet.

The snake on the ground, coloured like the ground, and shaped like the dead curved sticks or vines seen everywhere on the ground, and motionless like the vine, does not more closely assimilate to its surroundings than birds in trees often do—the birds which the Indian must also see. A stranger in these regions, even the naturalist with a sight quickened by enthusiasm, finds it hard to detect a parrot in a lofty tree, even when he knows that parrots are there; for their greenness in the green foliage, and the correlated habit they possess of remaining silent and motionless in the presence of an intruder, make them invisible to him, and he is astonished that the Indian should be able to detect them. The Indian knows how to look for them; it is his trade, which is long to learn; but he is obliged to learn it, for his success in life, and even life itself, depends on it, since in the savage state Nature kills those who fail in her competitive examinations.

The reader has doubtless often seen those little picture-puzzles, variously labelled "Where's the Cat?" or "Mad Bull," or" Burglar," or "Policeman," or "Snake in the Grass," etc., in which the thing named and to be discovered is formed by branches and foliage, and by running water, and drapery, and lights and shadows in the sketch. At first one finds it extremely difficult to detect this picture within a picture; and at last—with the suddenness with which one invariably detects a dull-coloured snake, seen previously but not distinguished—the object sought for appears, and is thereafter so plain to the eye that one cannot look at the sketch, even held at a distance, without seeing the cat, or policeman, or whatever it happens to be. And after patiently studying some scores or hundreds of these puzzles one gets to know just how to find the thing concealed, and finds it quickly—almost at a glance at last. Now the ingenious person that first invented this pretty puzzle probably had no thought of Nature, with her curious imitative and protective resemblances, in his mind; yet he might very well have taken the hint from Nature, for this is what she does. The animal that must be seen to be avoided, and the animal that must be seen to be taken, are there in her picture, sketched in with such cunning art that to the uninstructed eye they form only portions of branch and foliage and shadow and sunlight above, and dull-hued or variegated earth and stones and dead and withering herbage underneath.

It is possible that slight differences may exist in the seeing powers of different nations, due to the effect of physical conditions: thus, the inhabitants of mountainous districts and of dry elevated table lands may have a better sight than dwellers in low, humid, and level regions, although just the reverse may be the case. Among European nations the Germans are generally supposed to have weak eyes, owing, some imagine, to their excessive indulgence in tobacco; while others attribute the supposed decay to the form of type used in their books, which requires closer looking at than ours in reading. That they will deteriorate still further in this direction, and from being a spectacled people become a blind one, to the joy of their enemies, is not likely to happen, and probably the decadence has been a great deal exaggerated. Animals living in darkness become near-sighted, and then nearer-sighted still, and so on progressively until the vanishing point is reached. In a community or nation a similar decline might begin from much reading of German books, or perpetual smoking of pipes with big china bowls, or from some other unknown cause; but the decay could not progress far, because there is nothing in man to take the place of sight, as there is in the blind cave rats and fishes and insects. And if we could survey mankind from China to Peru with all the scientific appliances which are brought to bear on the Board-school children in London, and on the nation generally, the differences in the powers of vision in the various races, nations, and tribes, would probably appear very insignificant. The mistake which eye specialists and writers on the eye make is that they think too much about the eye. When they affirm that the conditions of our civilization are highly injurious to the sight, do they mean all the million conditions, or sets of conditions, embraced by our system, with the infinite variety of occupations and modes of living which men have, from the lighthouse-keeper to the worker underground, whose day is the dim glimmer of a miner's lamp? "An organ exercised beyond its wont will grow, and thus meet increase of demand by increase of supply," Herbert Spencer says; but, he adds, there is a limit soon reached, beyond which it is impossible to go. This increase of demand with us is everywhere—now on this organ and now on that, according to our work and way of life, and the eye is in no worse case than the other organs. There are among us many cases of heart complaint; civilization, in such cases, has put too great a strain on that organ, and it has reached the limit beyond which it cannot go. And so with the eye. The total number of the defective among us is no doubt very large, for we know that our system of life retards—it cannot effectually prevent—the healthy action of natural selection. Nature pulls one way and we pull the other, compassionately trying to save the unfit from the consequences of their unfitness. The humane instinct compels us; but the cruel instinct of the savage is less painful to contemplate than that mistaken or perverted compassion which seeks to perpetuate unfitness, and in the interest of suffering individuals inflicts a lasting injury on the race. It is a beautiful and sacred thing to minister to the blind, and to lead them, but a horrible thing to encourage them to marry and transmit the miserable defective condition to their posterity. Yet this is very common; and not long ago a leader-writer in one of the principal London journals spoke of this very thing in terms of rapturous approval, and looked forward to the growth of a totally blind race of men among us, as though it were something to be proud of—a triumph of our civilization!

Pelleschi, in his admirable book on the Chaco Indians, says that malformations are never seen in these savages, that physically they are all perfect men; and he remarks that in their exceedingly hard struggle for existence in a thorny wilderness, beset with perils, any bodily defect or ailment would be fatal. And as the eye in their life is the most important organ, it must be an eye without flaw. In this circumstance only do savages differ from us—namely, in the absence or rarity

VIEWING A DISTANT OBJECT

of defective eyes among them; and when those who, like Dr. Brudenell Carter, believe in the decadence of the eye in civilized man quote Humboldt's words about the miraculous sight of South American savages, they quote an error. It is not strange that Humboldt should have fallen into it, for, after all, he had only the means which we all possess of finding out things—a limited sight and a fallible mind. Like the savage, he had trained his faculties to observe and infer, and his inferences, like those of the savage, were sometimes wrong.

The savage sight is no better than ours for the simple reason that a better is not required. Nature has given to him, as to all her creatures, only what was necessary, and nothing for ostentation. Standing on the ground, his horizon is a limited one; and the animals he preys on, if often sharper-eyed and swifter than he, are without intelligence, and thus things are made equal. He can see the rhea as far as the rhea can see him; and if he possessed the eagle's far-seeing faculty it would be of no advantage to him. The high-soaring eagle requires to see very far, but the low-flying owl is near-sighted. And so on through the whole animal world: each kind has sight sufficient to find its food and escape from its enemies, and nothing beyond. Animals that live close to the surface have a very limited sight. Moreover, other faculties may usurp the eye's place, or develop so greatly as to make the eye of only secondary importance as an organ of intelligence. The snake offers a curious case. No other sense seems to have developed in it, yet I take the snake to be one of the nearest-sighted creatures in existence. From long observation of them I am convinced that small snakes of very sluggish habits do not see distinctly farther than from one to three yards. But the sluggish snake is the champion faster in the animal world, and can afford to lie quiescent until the wind of chance blows something eatable in its way; hence it does not require to see an object distinctly until almost within striking distance. Another remarkable case is that of the armadillo. Of two species I can confidently say that, if they are not blind, they are next door to blindness; yet they are diurnal animals that go abroad in the full glare of noon and wander far in search of food. But their sense of smell is marvellously acute, and, as in the case of the mole, it has made sight superfluous. To come back to man: if, in a state of nature, he is able to guess the character of objects nine times in ten, or nineteen in twenty, seen as far as he requires to see anything, his intellectual faculties make a better sight unnecessary. If the armadillo's scent had not been so keen, and man had not been gifted with nimble brains, the sight in both cases would have been vastly stronger; but the sharpening of its sense of smell has dimmed the armadillo's eyes and made him blinder than a snake; while man (from no fault of his own) is unable to see farther than the wolf and the ostrich and the wild ass.

XII

CONCERNING EYES

WHITE, crimson, emerald green, shining golden yellow, are amongst the colours seen in the eyes of birds. In owls, herons, cormorants, and many other tribes, the brightly-tinted eye is incomparably the finest feature and chief glory. It fixes the attention at once, appearing like a splendid gem, for which the airy bird-body, with its graceful curves and soft tints, forms an appropriate setting. When the eye closes in death, the bird, except to the naturalist, becomes a mere bundle of dead feathers; crystal globes may be put into the empty sockets, and a bold life-imitating attitude given to the stuffed specimen; but the vitreous orbs shoot forth no life-like flames, the "passion and the fire whose fountains are within" have vanished, and the best work of the taxidermist, who has given a life to his bastard art, produces in the mind only sensations of irritation and disgust. In museums, where limited space stands in the way of any abortive attempts at copying nature too closely, the stuffer's work is endurable because useful; but in a drawing-room, who does not close his eyes or turn aside to avoid seeing a case of stuffed birds—those unlovely mementoes of death in their gay plumes? Who does not shudder, albeit not with fear, to see the wild cat, filled with straw, yawning horribly, and trying to frighten the spectator with its crockery glare? I shall never forget the first sight I had of the late Mr. Gould's collection of humming-birds (now in the National Museum), shown to me by the naturalist himself, who evidently took considerable pride in the work of his hands. I had just left tropical nature behind me across the Atlantic, and the unexpected meeting with a transcript of it in a dusty room in Bedford Square gave me a distinct shock. Those pellets of dead feathers, which had long ceased to sparkle and shine, stuck with wires—not invisible—over blossoming cloth and tinsel, bushes, how melancholy they made me feel!

Considering the bright colour and great splendour of some eyes, particularly in birds, it seems probable that in these cases the organ has a twofold use: first and chiefly, to see; secondly, to intimidate an adversary with those luminous mirrors, in which all the dangerous fury of a creature brought to bay is seen depicted. Throughout nature the dark eye predominates; and there is certainly a great depth of fierceness in the dark eye of a bird of prey; but its effect is less than that produced by the vividly-coloured eye, or even of the white eye of some raptorial species, as, for instance, of the common South American hawk, *Asturina pucherani*. Violent emotions are associated in our minds—possibly, also, in the minds of other species—with certain colours. Bright red seems the appropriate hue of anger—the poet Herbert even calls the rose "angrie and brave" on account of its hue—and the red or orange certainly expresses resentment better than the dark eye. Even a very slight spontaneous variation in the colouring of the irides might give an advantage to an individual for natural selection to act on; for we can see in almost any living creature that not only in its perpetual metaphorical struggle for existence is its life safeguarded in many ways; but when protective resemblances, flight, and instincts of concealment all fail, and it is compelled to engage in a real struggle with a living adversary, it is provided for such occasions with another set of defences. Language and attitudes of defiance come into play; feathers or hairs are erected; beaks snap and strike, or teeth are gnashed, and the mouth foams or spits; the body puffs out; wings are waved or feet stamped on the ground, and many other intimidating gestures of rage are practised. It is not possible to believe that the colouring of the crystal globes, towards which an opponents sight is first directed, and which most vividly exhibit the raging emotions within, can have been entirely neglected as a means of defence by the principle of selection in nature. For all these reasons I believe the bright-coloured eye is an improvement on the dark eye.

Man has been very little improved in this direction, the dark eye, except in the north of Europe, having been, until recent times, almost or quite universal. The blue eye does not seem to have any advantage for man in a state of nature, being mild where fierceness of expression is required; it is almost unknown amongst the inferior creatures; and only on the supposition that the appearance of the eye is less important to man's welfare than it is to that of other species, can we account for its survival in a branch of the human race.

Cerulean eyes; locks comparable in hue to the "yellow hair that floats on the eastern clouds," and a white body, like snow with a blush on it—what could Nature have been dreaming of when she gave such things to her rudest most savage humans! That they should have overcome dark-eyed races, and trod on their necks and ruined their works, strikes one as unnatural, and reads like a fable.

Little, however, as the human eye has of assuming it to have been dark originally, there is a great deal of spontaneous variation in individuals, light hazel and blue-grey being apparently the most variable. I have found curiously marked and spotted eyes not uncommon; in some instances the spots being so black, round, and large as to produce the appearance of eyes with clusters of pupils on them. I have known one person with large brown spots on light blue-grey eyes, whose children all inherited the peculiarity; also another with reddish hazel irides thickly marked with fine characters resembling Greek letters. This person was an Argentine of Spanish blood, and was called by his neighbours *ojos escritos* or written eyes. It struck me as a very curious circumstance that the eyes, both in their ground colour and the form and disposition of the markings traced on them, were precisely like the eyes of a species of grebe, common in La Plata. Browning had perhaps observed eyes of this kind in some person he had met, when he makes his magician say to Pietro de Abano:

> Mark within my eyes its iris mystic-lettered—
> That's my name!

But we look in vain amongst men for the splendid crimson, flaming yellow, or startling white orbs which would have made the dark-skinned brave, inspired by violent emotions, a being terrible to see. Nature has neglected man in this respect, and it is to remedy the omission that he stains his face with bright pigments and crowns his head with eagles' barred plumes.

The quality of shining in the dark, seen in the eyes of many nocturnal and semi-nocturnal species, has always, I believe, a hostile purpose. When found in inoffensive species, as, for instance, in the lemurs, it can only be attributed to mimicry, and this would be a parallel case with butterflies mimicking the brilliant "warning colours" of other species on which birds do not prey. Cats amongst mammals, and owls amongst birds, have been most highly favoured; but to the owls the palm must be given. The feline eyes, as of puma or wild cat, blazing with wrath, are wonderful to see; sometimes the sight of them affects one like an electric shock; but for intense brilliance and quick changes, the dark orbs kindling with the startling suddenness of a cloud illumined by flashes of lightning, the yellow globes of the owl are unparalleled. Some readers might think my language exaggerated. Descriptions of bright sun sets and of storms with thunder and lightning would, no doubt, sound extravagant to one who had never witnessed these phenomena. Those only who spend years "conversing with wild animals in desert places," to quote Azara's words, know that, as with the atmosphere, so with animal life, there are special moments; and that a creature presenting a very sorry appearance dead in a museum, or living in captivity, may, when hard pressed and fighting for life in its own fastness, he sublimed by its fury into a weird and terrible object.

Nature has many surprises for those who wait on her; one of the greatest she ever favoured me with was the sight of a wounded Magellanic eagle-owl I shot in Patagonia. The haunt of this bird was an island in the river, overgrown with giant grasses and tall willows, leafless now, for it was in the middle of winter. Here I sought for and found him waiting on his perch for the sun to set. He eyed me so calmly when I aimed my gun, I scarcely had the heart to pull the trigger. He had reigned there so long, the feudal tyrant of that remote wilderness! Many a water-rat, stealing like a shadow along the margin between the deep stream and the giant rushes, he had snatched away to death; many a spotted wild pigeon had woke on its perch at night with his cruel crooked talons piercing its flesh; and beyond the valley on the bushy uplands many a crested tinamou had been slain on her nest and her beautiful glossy dark green eggs left to grow pale in the sun and wind, the little lives that were in them dead because of their mother's death. But I wanted that bird badly, and hardened my heart; the "demoniacal laughter" with which he had so often answered the rushing sound of the swift black river at eventide would be heard no more. I fired; he swerved on his perch, remained suspended for a few moments, then slowly fluttered down. Behind the spot where he had fallen was a great mass of tangled dark-green grass, out of which rose the tall, slender boles of the trees; overhead through the fretwork of leafless twigs the sky was flushed with tender roseate tints, for the sun had now gone down and the surface of the earth was in shadow. There, in such a scene, and with the wintry quiet of the desert over it all, I found my victim stung by his wounds to fury and prepared for the last

MAGELLANIC EAGLE-OWL

supreme effort. Even in repose he is a big eagle-like bird; now his appearance was quite altered, and in the dim, uncertain light he looked gigantic in size—a monster of strange form and terrible aspect. Each particular feather stood out on end, the tawny barred tail spread out like a fan, the immense tiger-coloured wings wide open and rigid, so that as the bird, that had clutched the grass with his great feathered claws, swayed his body slowly from side to side as a snake about to strike sways his head, or as an angry watchful cat moves its tail—first the tip of one, then of the other wing touched the ground. The black hams stood erect, while in the centre of the wheel-shaped head the beak snapped incessantly, producing a sound resembling the clicking of a sewing-machine. This was a suitable setting for the pair of magnificent furious eyes, on which I gazed with a kind of fascination, not unmixed with fear when I remembered the agony of pain suffered on former occasions from sharp, crooked talons driven into me to the bone. The irides were of a bright orange colour, but every time I attempted to approach the bird they kindled into great globes of quivering yellow flame, the black pupils being surrounded by a scintillating crimson light which threw out minute yellow sparks into the air. When I retired from the bird this preternatural fiery aspect would instantly vanish.

The dragon eyes of that Magellanic owl haunt me still, and when I remember them, the bird's death still weighs on my conscience, albeit by killing it I bestowed on it that dusty immortality which is the portion of stuffed specimens in a museum.

The question as to the cause of this fiery appearance is one hard to answer. We know that the source of the luminosity in owls' and cats' eyes is the *tapedum lucidum*—the light-reflecting membrane between the retina and the sclerotic coat of the eyeball; but the mystery remains. When with the bird, I particularly noticed that every time I retired the nictitating membrane would immediately cover the eyes and obscure them for some time, as they will when an owl is confronted with strong sunlight; and this gave me the impression that the fiery, flashing appearance was accompanied with, or followed by, a burning or smarting sensation. I will here quote a very suggestive passage from a letter on this subject written to me by a gentleman of great attainments in science: "Eyes certainly do shine in the dark—some eyes, *e.g.* those of cats and owls; and the scintillation you speak of is probably another form of the phenomenon. It probably depends upon some extra-sensibility of the retina analogous to what exists in the molecular constitution of sulphide of calcium and other phosphorescent substances. The difficulty is in the *scintillation*. We know that light of this character has its source in the heat vibrations of molecules at the temperature of incandescence, and the electric light is no exception to the rule. A possible explanation is that supra-sensitive retinæ in times of excitement become increasedly phosphorescent and the same excitement causes a change in the curvature of the lens, so that the light is focussed, and *pro tanto* brightened into sparks. Seeing how little we know of natural forces, it may be that what we call light in such a case is eye speaking to eye—an emanation from the window of one brain into the window of another."

Probably all those cases one hears and reads about—some historical—of human eyes flashing fire and blazing with wrath, are mere poetic exaggerations. One would not look for these fiery eyes amongst the peaceful children of civilization, who, when they make war, do so without anger, and kill their enemies by machinery, without even seeing them; but amongst savage or semi-savage men, carnivorous in their diet, fierce in disposition, and extremely violent in their passions. It is precisely amongst people of this description that I have lived a great deal. I have often seen them frenzied with excitement, their faces white as ashes, hair erect, and eyes drooping great tears of rage, but I have never seen anything in them even approaching to that fiery appearance described in the owl.

Nature has done comparatively little for the human eye, not only in denying it the terrifying splendours found in some other species, but also in the minor merit of beauty. When going about the world one cannot help thinking that the various races and tribes of men, differing in the colour of their skins and in the climates and conditions they live in, ought to have differently-coloured eyes. In Brazil, I was greatly struck with the magnificent appearance of many of the negro women I saw there; well-formed, tall, majestic creatures, often appropriately clothed in loose white gowns and white turban-like headdresses; while on their round polished blue-black arms they wore silver armlets. It seemed to me that pale golden irides, as in the intensely black tyrant-bird *Lichenops perspicillata*, would have given a finishing glory to these sable beauties, completing their strange unique loveliness. Again in that exquisite type of female beauty which we see in the white girl with a slight infusion of negro blood, giving the graceful frizzle to the hair, the purple-red hue to the lips, and the delicate dusky terra-cotta tinge to the skin, an eye more suitable than the dark dull brown would have been the intense orange-brown seen in some lemur's eyes. For many very dark-skinned tribes nothing more beautiful than the ruby-red iris could be imagined; while sea-green eyes would have best suited dusky-pale Polynesians and languid peaceful tribes like the one described in Tennyson's poem:

> And round about the keel with faces pale,
> Dark faces pale against that rosy flame,
> The mild-eyed melancholy Lotos-eaters came.

Since we cannot have the eyes we should like best to have, let us consider those that Nature has given us. The incomparable beauty of the "emerald eye" has been greatly praised by the poets, particularly by those of Spain. Emerald eyes, if they only existed, would certainly be beautiful beyond all others, especially if set off with dark or black hair and that dim pensive creamy pallor of the skin frequently seen in warm climates, and which is more beautiful than the rosy complexion prevalent in northern regions, though not so lasting. But either they do not exist or else I have been very unfortunate, for after long seeking I am compelled to confess that never yet have I been gratified by the sight of emerald eyes. I have seen eyes called green, that is, eyes with a greenish tinge or light in them, but they were not the eyes I sought. One can easily forgive the poets their misleading descriptions, since they are not trustworthy guides, and very often, like Humpty Dumpty in *Through the Looking Glass*, make words do "extra work." For sober fact one is accustomed to look to men of science; yet, strange to say, while these complain that we—the unscientific ones—are without any settled and correct ideas about the colour of our own eyes, they have endorsed the poet's fable, and have even taken considerable pains to persuade the world of its truth. Dr. Paul Broca is their greatest authority. In his *Manual for Anthropologists* he divides human eyes into four distinct types—orange, green, blue, grey; and these four again into five varieties each. The symmetry of such a classification suggests at once that it is an arbitrary one. Why orange, for instance? Light hazel, clay colour, red, dull brown, cannot properly be called orange; but the division requires the five supposed varieties of the dark pigmented eye to be grouped under one name, and because there is yellow pigment in some dark eyes they are all called orange. Again, to make the five grey varieties the lightest grey is made so very light that only when placed on a sheet of white paper does it show grey at all; but there is always some colour in the human skin, so that Broca's eye would appear absolutely white by contrast—a thing unheard of in nature. Then we have the green, beginning with the palest sage green, and up through grass green and emerald green, to the deepest sea green and the green of the holly leaf. Do such eyes exist in nature? In theory they do. The blue eye is blue, and the grey grey, because in such eyes there is no yellow or brown pigment on the outer surface of the iris to prevent the dark purple pigment—the *uvea*—on the inner surface from being seen through the membrane, which has different degrees of opacity, making the eye appear grey, light or dark blue, or purple, as the case may be. When yellow pigment is deposited in small quantity on the outer membrane, then it should, according to the theory, blend with the inner blue and make green. Unfortunately for the anthropologists, it doesn't. It only gives in some cases the greenish variable tinge I have mentioned, but nothing approaching to the decided greens of Broca's tables. Given an eye with the right degree of translucency in the membrane and a very thin deposit of yellow pigment spread equally over the surface, the result would be a perfectly green iris. Nature, however, does not proceed quite in this way. The yellow pigment varies greatly in hue; it is muddy yellow, brown, or earthy colour, and it never spreads itself uniformly over the surface, but occurs in patches grouped about the pupil and spreads in dull rays or lines and spots, so that the eye which science says "ought to be called green" is usually a very dull blue-grey, or brownish-blue, or clay colour, and in some rare instances shows a changeable greenish hue.

In the remarks accompanying the Report of the Anthropometric Committee of the British Association 1881 and 1883, it is said that green eyes are more common than the tables indicate, and that eyes that should properly be called green, owing to the popular prejudice against that term, have been recorded as grey or some other colour.

Does any such prejudice exist? or is it necessary to go about with the open manual in our hands to know a green eye when we see one? No doubt the "popular prejudice" is supposed to have its origin in Shakespeare's description of jealousy as a green-eyed monster; but if Shakespeare has any great weight with the popular mind, the prejudice ought to be the other way, since he is one of those who sing the splendours of the green eye.

Thus in *Romeo and Juliet*:

> The eagle, madam,
> Hath not so green, so quick, so fair an eye
> As Paris hath.

The lines are, however, nonsense, as green-eyed eagles have no existence; and perhaps the question of the popular prejudice is not worth arguing about.

Once only in my long years' quest after green eyes, during which I have sometimes walked miles along a crowded thoroughfare seeing the orbs of every person that passed me, was I led to think that my reward had come at last. On taking my seat in a public conveyance I noticed a fashionably-dressed lady, of a singularly attractive appearance, on the opposite seat, but a little higher up. Her skin was somewhat pale, her hair dark, and her eyes green! "At last!" I exclaimed, mentally, glad as if I had found a priceless gem. It was misery to me to have to observe her furtively, to think that I should so soon lose sight of her! Several minutes passed, during which she did not move her head, and still the eyes were green—not one of the dull and dark hues that Broca imagined and painted, but a clear, exquisitely beautiful sea-green, as sea-water looks with a strong sunlight in it, where it is deep and pure, in the harbour of some rocky island under the tropics. At length, not yet convinced, I moved a little higher up on my seat, so that when I should next look at her, her eyes would meet mine full and straight. The wished (and feared) moment came: alas! the eyes were no longer green, but grey, and not very pure in colour. Having looked green when viewed obliquely, they could not be a very pure grey: they were simply grey eyes with an exceedingly thin pigment, so thin as not to appear as pigment, equally spread over the surface of the irides. This made the eyes in some lights appear green, just as a dog's eyes, when the animal sits in shadow and the upturned balls catch the light, sometimes look pure green. I know a dog, now living, whose eyes in such circumstances always appear of that colour. But as a rule the dog's eyes take a hyaline blue.

If we could leave out the mixed or neutral eyes, which are in a transitional state—blue eyes with some pigment obscuring their blueness, and making them quite unclassifiable, as no two pairs of eyes are found alike—then all eyes might be divided into two great natural orders, those with and those without pigment on the outer surface of the membrane. They could not well be called light and dark eyes, since many hazel eyes are really lighter than purple and dark grey eyes. They might, however, be simply called brown and blue, for in all eyes with the outer pigment there is brown, or something scarcely distinguishable from brown; and all eyes without pigment, even the purest greys, have some blueness.

Brown eyes express animal passions rather than intellect and the higher moral feelings. They are frequently equalled in their own peculiar kind of eloquence by the brown or dark eyes in the domestic dog. In animals there is, in fact, often an exaggerated eloquence of expression. To judge from their eyes, caged cats and eagles in the Zoological Gardens are all furred and feathered Bonnivards. Even in the most intellectual of men the brown eye speaks more of the heart than of the head. In the inferior creatures the black eye is always keen and cunning or else soft and mild, as in fawns, doves, aquatic birds, etc.; and it is remarkable that in man also the black eye—dark brown iris with large pupil—generally has one or the other of these predominant expressions. Of course, in highly civilized communities, individual exceptions are extremely numerous. Spanish and negro women have wonderfully soft and loving eyes, while the cunning weasel-like eye is common everywhere, especially amongst Asiatics. In high-caste Orientals the keen, cunning look has been refined and exalted to an appearance of marvellous subtlety—the finest expression of which the black eye is capable.

The blue eye—all blues and greys being here included—is *par excellence* the eye of intellectual man: that outer warm-coloured pigment hanging like a cloud, as it were, over the brain absorbs its most spiritual emanations, so that only when it is quite blown away are we able to look into the soul, forgetting man's kinship with the brutes. When one is unaccustomed to it from always living with dark-eyed races, the blue eye seems like an anomaly in nature, if not a positive blunder; for its power of expressing the lower and commonest instincts and passions of our race is comparatively limited; and in cases where the higher faculties are undeveloped it seems vacant and meaningless. Add to this that the ethereal blue colour is associated in the mind with atmospheric phenomena rather than with solid matter, inorganic or animal. It is the hue of the void, expressionless sky; of shadows on far-off hill and cloud; of water under certain conditions of the atmosphere, and of the unsubstantial summer haze,

> whose margin fades
> For ever and for ever as I move.

In organic nature we only find the hue sparsely used in the quickly-perishing flowers of some frail plants; while a few living things of free and buoyant motions, like birds and butterflies, have been touched on the wings with the celestial tint only to make them more aerial in appearance. Only in man, removed from the gross materialism of nature, and in whom has been developed the highest faculties of the mind, do we see the full beauty and significance of the blue eye—the eye, that is, without the interposing cloud of dark pigment covering it. In the biography of Nathaniel Hawthorne, the author says of him: "His eyes were large, dark-blue, brilliant, and full of varied expression. Bayard Taylor used to say that they were the only eyes he ever knew to flash fire... While he was yet at college, an old gipsy woman, meeting him suddenly in a woodland path, gazed at him and asked:

"'Are you a man, or an angel?'"

I may say here that gipsies are so accustomed to concentrate their sight on the eyes of the people they meet that they acquire a marvellous proficiency in detecting their expression; they study them with an object, as my friend the gambler studied the backs of the cards he played with; without seeing the eyes of their intended dupe they would be at a loss what to say.

To return to Hawthorne. His wife says in one of her letters quoted in the book: "The flame of his eyes consumed compliment, cant, sham, and falsehood; while the most wretched sinners—so many of whom came to confess to him—met in his glance such a pity and sympathy that they ceased to be afraid of God and began to return to Him......*I never dared gaze at him, even I, unless his lids were down.*"

I think we have, most of us, seen eyes like these—eyes which one rather avoids meeting, because when met one is startled by the sight of a naked human soul brought so near. One person, at least, I have known to whom the above description would apply in every particular; a man whose intellectual and moral nature was of the highest order, and who perished at the age of thirty, a martyr to the cause of humanity.

How very strange, then, that savage man should have been endowed with this eye unsuited to express the instincts and passions of savages, but able to express the intelligence, high moral feelings, and spirituality which a humane civilization was, long ages after, to develop in his torpid brain! A fact like this seems to fit in with that flattering, fascinating, ingenious hypothesis invented by Wallace to account for facts which, according to the theory of natural selection, ought not to exist.

In answer to the question, What is the colour of the British eye? so frequently asked, and not yet definitely settled, I wish, in conclusion, to record my own observations here. I have remarked a surprisingly great difference in the eyes of the two classes into which the population is practically divisible—the well-to-do class and the poor. I began my observations in London—there is no better place; and my simple plan was to walk along the most frequented streets and thoroughfares, observing the eyes of every person that passed me. My sight being good, even the very brief glance, which was all that could be had in most cases, was sufficient for my purpose; and in this way hundreds of pairs of eyes could be seen in the course of a day. In Cheapside the population seemed too mixed; but in Piccadilly, and Bond Street, and along Rotten Row, during the season, it appeared safe to set down a very large majority of the pedestrians as belonging to the prosperous class. There are other streets and thoroughfares in London where very nearly all the people seen in it at any time are of the working class. I also frequently strolled up and down the long streets, where the poor do their marketing on Saturday evenings, and when, owing to the slow rate of progress, their features can be easily studied.

To take the better class first. I think it would puzzle any stranger, walking in Piccadilly or along the Row on a spring afternoon, to say what the predominant colour of the English eye is, so great is the variety. Every shade of grey and blue, from the faint cerulean of a pale sky, to the ultramarine, called purple and violet, and which looks black; and every type and shade of the dark eye, from the lightest hazel and the yellowish tint resembling that of the sheep's iris, to the deepest browns, and the iris of liquid jet with ruddy and orange reflections in it—the tortoiseshell eye and chief glory of the negro woman. Another surprising fact was the large proportion of fine eyes. For this variety and excellence several explanations might be given, not one of which would probably seem quite satisfactory; I therefore leave the reader to form his own theory on the subject.

In the lower class no such difficulty appeared. Here, in a very large majority of cases—about eighty per cent I think—the eye was grey, or grey-blue, but seldom pure. The impurity was caused by a small quantity of pigment, as I could generally see by looking closely at the iris, a yellowish tinge being visible round the pupil. My conclusion was, that this impure grey eye is the typical British eye at the present time; that it is becoming pigmented, and will probably, if the race endures long enough, become dark.

XIII

THE PLAINS OF PATAGONIA

NEAR the end of Darwin's famous narrative of the voyage of the *Beagle* there is a passage which, for me, has a very special interest and significance. It is as follows, and the italicization is mine: "In calling up images of the past, I find the plains of Patagonia frequently cross before my eyes; yet these plains are pronounced by all to be most wretched and useless. They are characterized only by negative possessions; without habitations, without water, without trees, without mountains, they support only a few dwarf plants. *Why, then—and the case is not peculiar to myself—have these arid wastes taken so firm possession of my mind?* Why have not the still more level, the greener and more fertile pampas, which are serviceable to mankind, produced an equal impression? I can scarcely analyze these feelings, but it must be partly owing to the free scope given to the imagination. The plains of Patagonia are boundless, for they are scarcely practicable, and hence unknown; they bear the stamp of having thus lasted for ages, and there appears no limit to their duration through future time. If, as the ancients supposed, the flat earth was surrounded by an impassable breadth of water, or by deserts heated to an intolerable excess, who would not look at these last boundaries to man's knowledge with deep but ill-defined sensations?"

That he did not in this passage hit on the right explanation of the sensations he experienced in Patagonia, and of the strength of the impressions it made on his mind, I am quite convinced; for the thing is just as true of to-day as of the time, in 1836, when he wrote that the case was not peculiar to himself. Yet since that date—which now, thanks to Darwin, seems so remote to the naturalist— those desolate regions have ceased to be impracticable, and, although still uninhabited and uninhabitable, except to a few nomads, they are no longer unknown. During the last twenty years the country has been crossed in various directions, from the Atlantic to the Andes, and from the Rio Negro to the Straits of Magellan, and has been found all barren. The mysterious illusive city, peopled by whites, which was long believed to exist in the unknown interior, in a valley called Trapalanda, is to moderns a myth, a mirage of the mind, as little to the traveller's imagination as the glittering capital of great Manoa, which Alouzo Pizarro and his false friend Orellana failed to discover. The traveller of to-day really expects to see nothing more exciting than a solitary huanaco keeping watch on a hilltop, and a few grey-plumaged rheas flying from him, and, possibly, a band of long-haired roving savages, with their faces painted black and red. Yet, in spite of accurate knowledge, the old charm still exists in all its freshness; and after all the discomforts and sufferings endured in a desert cursed with eternal barrenness, the returned traveller finds in after years that it still keeps its hold on him, that it shines brighter in memory, and is dearer to him than any other region he may have visited.

We know that the more deeply our feelings are moved by any scene the more vivid and lasting will its image be in memory—a fact which accounts for the comparatively unfading character of the images that date back to the period of childhood, when we are most emotional. Judging from my own case, I believe that we have here the secret of the persistence of Patagonian images, and their frequent recurrence in the hinds of many who have visited that grey, monotonous, and, in one sense, eminently uninteresting region. It is not the effect of the unknown, it is not imagination; it is that nature in these desolate scenes, for a reason to be guessed at by-and-by, moves us more deeply than in others. In describing his rambles in one of the most desolate spots in Patagonia, Darwin remarks: "Yet, in passing over these scenes, without one bright object near, an ill-defined but strong sense of pleasure is vividly excited." When I recall a Patagonian scene, it comes before me so complete in all its vast extent, with all its details so clearly outlined, that, if I were actually gazing on it, I could scarcely see it more distinctly; yet other scenes, even those that were beautiful and sublime, with forest, and ocean, and mountain, and over all the deep blue sky and brilliant sunshine of the tropics, appear no longer distinct and entire in memory, and only become more broken and clouded if any attempt is made to regard them attentively. Here and there I see a wooded mountain, a grove of palms, a flowery tree, green waves dashing on a rocky shore—nothing but isolated patches of bright colour, the parts of the picture that have not faded on a great blurred canvas, or series of canvases. These last are images of scenes which were looked on with wonder and admiration—feelings which the Patagonian wastes could not inspire—but the grey, monotonous solitude woke other and deeper feelings, and in that mental state the scene was indelibly impressed on the mind.

I spent the greater part of one winter at a point on the Rio Negro, seventy or eighty miles from the sea, where the valley on my side of the water was about five miles wide. The valley alone was habitable where, there was water for man and beast, and a thin soil producing grass and grain; it is perfectly level, and ends abruptly at the foot of the bank or terrace-like formation of the higher barren plateau. It was my custom to go out every morning on horseback with my gun, and, followed by one dog, to ride away from the valley; and no sooner would I climb the terrace and plunge into the grey universal thicket, than I would find myself as completely alone and cut off from all sight and sound of human occupancy as if five hundred instead of only five miles separated me from the hidden green valley and river. So wild and solitary and remote seemed that grey waste, stretching away into infinitude, a waste untrodden by man, and where the wild animals are so few that they have made no discoverable path in the wilderness of thorns. There I might have dropped down and died, and my flesh been devoured by birds, and my bones bleached white in sun and wind, and no person would have found them, and it would have been forgotten that one had ridden forth in the morning and had not returned. Or if, like the few wild animals there—puma, huanaco, and hare-like *Dolichotis*, or Darwin's rhea and the crested tinamou among the birds—I had been able to exist without water, I might have made myself a hermitage of brushwood or dug-out in the side of a cliff, and dwelt there until I had grown grey as the stones and trees around me, and no human foot would have stumbled on my hiding-place.

Not once, nor twice, nor thrice, but day after day I returned to this solitude, going to it in the morning as if to attend a festival, and leaving it only when hunger and thirst and the westering sun compelled me. And yet I had no object in going— no motive which could be put into words; for although I carried a gun, there was nothing to shoot—the shooting was all left behind in the valley. Sometimes a *Dolichotis*, starting up at my approach, flashed for one moment on my sight, to vanish the next moment in the continuous thicket; or a covey of tinamous sprang rocket-like into the air, and fled away with long wailing notes and loud whur of wings; or on some distant hill-side a bright patch of yellow, of a deer that was watching me, appeared and remained motionless for two or three minutes. But the animals were few, and sometimes I would pass an entire day without seeing one mammal, and perhaps not more than a dozen birds of any size. The weather at that time was cheerless, generally with a grey film of cloud spread over the sky, and a bleak wind, often cold enough to make my bridle hand feel quite numb. Moreover, it was not possible to enjoy a canter; the bushes grew so close together that it was as much as one could do to pass through at a walk without brushing against them; and at this slow pace, which would have seemed intolerable in other circumstances, I would ride about for hours at a stretch. In the scene itself there was nothing to delight the eye. Everywhere through the light, grey mould, grey as ashes and formed by the ashes of myriads of generations of dead trees, where the wind had blown on it, or the rain had washed it away, the underlying yellow sand appeared, and the old ocean-polished pebbles, dull red, and grey, and green, and yellow. On arriving at a hill, I would slowly ride to its summit, and stand there to survey the prospect. On every side it stretched away in great undulations; but the undulations were wild and irregular; the hills were rounded and cone-shaped, they were solitary and in groups and ranges; some sloped gently, others were ridge-like and stretched away in league-long terraces, with other terraces beyond; and all alike were clothed in the grey everlasting thorny vegetation. How grey it all was! hardly less so near at hand than on the haze-wrapped horizon, where the hills were dim and the outline blurred by distance. Sometimes I would see the large eagle-like, white-breasted buzzard, *Buteo erythronotus*, perched on the summit of a bush half a mile away; and so long as it would continue stationed motionless before me my eyes would remain involuntarily fixed on it, just as one keeps his eyes on a bright light shining in the gloom; for the whiteness of the hawk seemed to exercise a fascinating power on the vision, so surpassingly bright was it by contrast in the midst of that universal unrelieved greyness. Descending from my look-out, I would take up my aimless wanderings again, and visit other elevations to gaze on the same landscape from another point; and so on for hours, and at noon I would dismount and sit or lie on my folded poncho for an hour or longer. One day, in these rambles, I discovered a small grove composed of twenty to thirty trees, about eighteen feet high, and taller than the surrounding trees. They were growing at a convenient distance apart, and had evidently been resorted to by a herd of deer or other wild animals for a very long time, for the boles were polished to a glassy smoothness with much rubbing, and the ground beneath was trodden to a floor of clean, loose yellow sand. This grove was on a hill differing in shape from other hills in its neighbourhood, so that it was easy for me to find it on other occasions; and after a time I made a point of finding and using it as a resting-place every day at noon. I did not ask myself why I made choice of that one spot, sometimes going miles out of my way to sit there, instead of sitting down under any one of the millions of trees and bushes covering the country, on any other hillside. I thought nothing at all about it, but acted unconsciously; only afterwards, when revolving the subject, it seemed to me that after having rested there once, each time I wished to rest again the wish came associated with the image of that particular clump of trees, with polished stems and clean bed of sand beneath; and in a short time I formed a habit of returning, animal-like, to repose at that same spot.

It was perhaps a mistake to say that I would sit down and rest, since I was never tired: and yet without being tired, that noonday pause, during which I sat for an hour without moving, was strangely grateful. All day the silence seemed grateful, it was very perfect, very profound. There were no insects, and the only bird-sound— a feeble chirp of alarm emitted by a small skulking wren-like species—was not heard oftener than two or three times an hour. The only sounds as I rode were the muffled hoof-strokes of my horse, scratching of twigs against my boot or saddle-flap, and the low panting of the dog. And it seemed to be a relief to escape even from these sounds when I dismounted and sat down: for in a few moments the dog would stretch his head out on his paws and go to sleep, and then there would be no sound, not even the rustle of a leaf. For unless the wind blows strong there is no fluttering motion and no whisper in the small stiff undeciduous leaves; and the bushes stand unmoving as if carved out of stone. One day while *listening* to the silence, it occurred to my mind to wonder what the effect would be if I were to shout aloud. This seemed at the time a horrible suggestion of fancy, a "lawless and uncertain thought" which almost made me shudder, and I was anxious to dismiss it quickly from my mind. But during those solitary days it was a rare thing for any thought to cross my mind; animal forms did not cross my vision or bird-voices assail my hearing more rarely. In that novel state of mind I was in, thought had become impossible. Elsewhere I had always been able to think most freely on horseback; and on the pampas, even in the most lonely places, my mind was always most active when I travelled at a swinging gallop. This was doubtless habit; but now, with a horse under me, I had become incapable of reflection: my mind had suddenly transformed itself from a thinking machine into a machine for some other unknown purpose. To think was like setting in motion a noisy engine in my brain; and there was something there which bade me be still, and I was forced to obey. My state was one of *suspense* and *watchfulness*: yet I had no expectation of meeting with an adventure, and felt as free from apprehension as I feel now when sitting in a room in London. The change in me was just as great and wonderful as if I had changed my identity for that of another man or animal; but at the time I was powerless to wonder at or speculate about it; the state seemed familiar rather than strange, and although accompanied by a strong feeling of elation, I did not know it—did not know that something had come between me and my intellect—until I lost it and returned to my former self—to thinking, and the old insipid existence.

Such changes in us, however brief in duration they may be, and in most cases they are very brief, but which so long as they last seem to affect us down to the very roots of our being, and come as a great surprise—a revelation of an unfamiliar and unsuspected nature hidden under the nature we are conscious of—can only be attributed to an instantaneous reversion to the primitive and wholly savage mental conditions. Probably not many men exist who would be unable to recall similar cases in their own experience; but it frequently happens that the revived instinct is so purely animal in character and repugnant to our refined or humanitarian feelings, that it is sedulously concealed and its promptings resisted. In the military and seafaring vocations, and in lives of travel and adventure, these sudden and surprising reversions are most frequently experienced. The excitement affecting men going into battle, which even affects those who are constitutionally timid and will cause them to exhibit a reckless daring and contempt of danger astonishing to themselves, is a familiar instance. This instinctive courage has been compared to intoxication, but it does not, like alcohol, obscure a man's faculties: on the contrary, he is far more keenly active to everything going on around him than the person who keeps perfectly cool. The man who is coolly courageous in fight has his faculties in their ordinary condition: the faculties of the man who goes into battle inflamed with instinctive, joyous excitement are sharpened to a preternatural keenness.[1] When the constitutionally timid man has had an experience of this kind he looks back on the day that brought it to him as the happiest he has known, one that stands out brightly and shines with a strange glory among his days.

When we are suddenly confronted with any terrible danger, the change of nature we undergo is equally great. In some cases fear paralyzes us, and, like animals, we stand still, powerless to move a step in flight, or to lift a hand in defence of our lives; and sometimes we are seized with panic, and, again, act more like the inferior animals than rational beings. On the other hand, frequently in cases of sudden extreme peril, which cannot be escaped by flight, and must be instantly faced, even the most timid men at once, as if by miracle, become possessed of the necessary courage, sharp, quick apprehension, and swift decision. This is a miracle very common in nature; man and the inferior animals alike, when confronted with almost certain death "gather resolution from despair." We are accustomed to call this the "courage of despair"; but there can really be no trace of so debilitating a feeling in the person fighting, or prepared to fight, for dear life. At such times the mind is clearer than it has ever been; the nerves are steel; there is nothing felt but a wonderful strength and fury and daring. Looking back at certain perilous moments in my own life, I remember them with a kind of joy; not that there was any joyful excitement then, but because they brought me a new experience—a new nature, as it were—and lifted me for a time above myself. And yet, comparing myself with other men, I find that on ordinary occasions my courage is rather below than above the average. And probably this instinctive courage, which flashes out so brightly on occasions, is inherited by a very large majority of the male children born into the world; only in civilized life the exact conjuncture of circumstances needed to call it into activity rarely occurs.

In hunting, again, instinctive impulses come very much to the surface. Leech caricatured Gallic ignorance of fox-hunting in England when he made his French gentleman gallop over the hounds and dash away to capture the fox himself; but the sketch may be also taken as a comic illustration of a feeling that exists in every one of us. If any sportsman among my readers has ever been confronted with some wild animal—a wild dog, a pig, or cat, let us say—when he had no firearm or other weapon to kill it in the usual civilized way, and has nevertheless attacked it, driven by a sudden uncontrollable impulse, with a hunting knife, or anything that came to hand, and has succeeded in slaying it, I would ask such a one whether this victory did not give him a greater satisfaction than all his other achievements in the field? After it, all legitimate sport would seem illegitimate, and whole hecatombs of hares and pheasants, and even large animals, fallen before his gun, would only stir in him a feeling of disgust and self-contempt. He would probably hold his tongue about a combat of that brutal kind, but all the same he would gladly remember how in some strange, unaccountable way he suddenly became possessed of the daring, quickness, and certitude necessary to hold his wily, desperate foe in check, to escape its fangs and claws, and finally to overcome it. Above all, he would remember the keen feeling of savage joy experienced in the contest. This would make all ordinary sport seem insipid; to kill a rat in some natural way would seem better to him than to murder elephants scientifically from a safe distance. The feeling occasionally bursts out in *The Story of My Heart*: "To shoot with a gun is nothing...Give me an iron mace that I may crush the savage beast and hammer him down. A spear to thrust him through with, so that I may feel the long blade enter, and the push of the shaft." And more in the same strain, shocking to some, perhaps, but showing that gentle Richard Jefferies had in him some of the elements of a fine barbarian.

But it is in childhood and boyhood, when instincts are nearest to the surface, and ready when occasion serves to spring into activity. Inherited second nature is weakest then; and habit has not progressed far in weaving its fine network of restraining influences over the primitive nature. The network is continually being strengthened in the individual's life, and, in the end he is cased, like the caterpillar, in an impervious cocoon; only, as we have seen, there are in life miraculous moments when the cocoon suddenly dissolves, or becomes transparent, and he is permitted to see himself in his original nakedness. The delight which children experience on entering woods and other wild places is very keen; and this feeling, although it diminishes as we advance in life, remains with us to the last. Equally great is their delight at finding wild fruits, honey, and other natural food; and even when not hungry they will devour it with strange zest. They will gladly feast on sour, acrid fruits, which at table, and picked in the garden, would only excite disgust. This instinctive seeking for food, and the delight experienced in finding it, occasionally comes up in very unexpected and surprising ways. "As I came through the wood," says Thoreau, "I caught a glimpse of a woodchuck stealing across my path, and felt a strange thrill of savage delight, and was strongly tempted to seize and devour him raw; not that I was hungry then, except for the wildness which he represented."

In almost all cases—those in which danger is encountered and rage experienced being exceptions—the return to an instinctive or primitive state of mind is accompanied by this feeling of elation, which, in the very young, rises to an intense gladness, and sometimes makes them mad with joy, like animals newly escaped from captivity. And, for a similar reason, the civilized life is one of continual repression, although it may not seem so until a glimpse of nature's wildness, a taste of adventure, an accident, suddenly makes it seem unspeakably irksome; and in that state we feel that our loss in departing from nature exceeds our gain.

It was elation of this kind, the feeling experienced on going back to a mental condition we have outgrown, which I had in the Patagonian solitude; for I had undoubtedly *gone back*; and that state of intense watchfulness, or alertness rather, with suspension of the higher intellectual faculties, represented the mental state of the pure savage. He thinks little, reasons little, having a surer guide in his instinct; he is in perfect harmony with nature, and is nearly on a level, mentally, with the wild animals he preys on, and which in their turn sometimes prey on him. If the plains of Patagonia affect a person in this way, even in a much less degree than in my case, it is not strange that they impress themselves so vividly on the mind, and remain fresh in memory, and return frequently; while other scenery, however grand or beautiful, fades gradually away, and is at last forgotten. To a slight, in most cases probably a very slight, extent, all natural sights and sounds affect us in the same way; but the effect is often transitory, and is gone with the first shock of pleasure, to be followed in some cases by a profound and mysterious melancholy. The greenness of earth; forest and river and hill; the blue haze and distant horizon; shadows of clouds sweeping over the sun-flushed landscape—to see it all is like returning to a home, which is more truly our home than any habitation we know. The cry of the wild bird pierces us to the heart; we have never heard that cry before, and it is more familiar to us than our mother's voice. "I heard," says Thoreau, "a robin in the distance, the first I had heard for many a thousand years, me thought, whose note I shall not forget for many a thousand more,—the same sweet and powerful song as of yore. O the evening robin!" Hafiz sings:

> O breeze of the morning blow me a memory of the ancient time;
> If after a thousand years thy odours should float o'er my dust,
> My bones, full of gladness uprising, would dance in the sepulchre!

And we ourselves are the living sepulchres of a dead past—that past which was ours for so many thousands of years before this life of the present began; its old bones are slumbering in us—dead, and yet not dead nor deaf to Nature's voices; the noisy burn, the roar of the waterfall, and thunder of long waves on the shore, and the sound of rain and whispering winds in the multitudinous leaves, bring it a memory of the ancient time; and the bones rejoice and dance in their sepulchre.

Professor W. K. Parker, in his work *On Mammalian Descent*, speaking of the hairy covering almost universal in this class of animals, says: "This has become, as every one knows, a custom among the race of men, and shows, at present, no sign of becoming obsolete. Moreover, that first correlation, namely, milk-glands and a hairy covering, appears to have entered the very soul of creatures of this class, and to have become *psychical* as well as *physical*, for in that type, which is only inferior to the angels, the fondness for this kind of outer covering is a strong and ineradicable passion." I am not sure that this view accords with some facts in our experience, and with some instinctive feelings which we all have. Like Waterton I have found that the feet take very kindly to the earth, however hot or cold or rough it may be, and that shoes, after being left off for a short time, seem as uncomfortable as a mask. The face is always uncovered; why does the supposed correlation not apply to this part? The face is pleasantly warm when the too delicate body shivers with cold under its covering; and pleasantly cool when the sun shines hot on us. When the wind strikes us on a hot day, or during violent exercise, the sensation to the face is extremely agreeable, but far from agreeable to the body where the covering does not allow the moisture to evaporate rapidly. The umbrella has not entered the soul—not yet; but it is miserable to get wet in the rain, yet pleasant to feel the rain on the face. "I am all face," the naked American savage said, to explain why he felt no discomfort from the bleak wind which made his civilized fellow-traveller shiver in his furs. Again, what a relief, what a pleasure, to throw off the clothes when occasion permits. Leigh Hunt wrote an amusing paper on the pleasures of going to bed, when the legs, long separated by unnatural clothing, delightedly rub against and renew their acquaintance with one another. Everyone knows the feeling. If it were convenient, and custom not so tyrannical, many of us would be glad to follow Benjamin Franklin's example, and rise not to dress, but to settle comfortably down to our morning's work, with nothing on. When, for the first time, in some region where nothing but a fig-leaf has "entered the soul," we see men and women going about naked and unashamed, we experience a slight shock; but it has more pleasure than pain in it, although we are reluctant to admit the pleasure, probably because we mistake the nature of the feeling. If, after seeing them for a few days in their native simplicity, our new friends appear before us clothed, we are shocked again, and this time disagreeably so; it is like seeing those who were free and joyous yesterday now appear with fettered feet and sullen downcast faces.

To leave this question; what has truly entered our soul and become psychical is our environment—that wild nature in which and to which we were born at an inconceivably remote period, and which made us what we are. It is true that we are eminently adaptive, that we have created, and exist in some sort of harmony with new conditions, widely different from those to which we were originally adapted; but the old harmony was infinitely more perfect than the new, and if there be such a thing as historical memory in us, it is not strange that the sweetest moment in any life, pleasant or dreary, should be when Nature draws near to it, and, taking up her neglected instrument, plays a fragment of some ancient melody, long unheard on the earth.

It might be asked: If nature has at times this peculiar effect on us, restoring instantaneously the old vanished harmony between organism and environment, why should it be experienced in a greater degree in the Patagonian desert than in other solitary places—a desert which is waterless, where animal voices are seldom heard, and vegetation is grey instead of green? I can only suggest a reason for the effect being so much greater in my own case. In sub-tropical woods and thickets, and in wild forests in temperate regions, the cheerful verdure and bright colours of flower and insects, if we have acquired a habit of looking closely at these things, and the melody and noises of bird-life engages the

THE PLAINS OF PATAGONIA

senses; there is movement and brightness; new forms, animal and vegetable, are continually appearing, curiosity and expectation are excited, and the mind is so much occupied with novel objects that the effect of wild nature in its entirety is minimized. In Patagonia the monotony of the plains, or expanse of low hills, the universal unrelieved greyness of everything, and the absence of animal forms and objects new to the eye, leave the mind open and free to receive an impression of visible nature as a whole. One gazes on the prospect as on the sea, for it stretches away sea-like, without change, into infinitude; but without the sparkle of water, the changes of hue which shadows and sunlight and nearness and distance give, and motion of waves and white flash of foam. It has a look of antiquity, of desolation, of eternal peace, of a desert that has been a desert from of old and will continue a desert for ever; and we know that its only human inhabitants are a few wandering savages, who live by hunting as their progenitors have done for thousands of years. Again, in fertile savannahs and pampas there may appear no signs of human occupancy, but the traveller knows that eventually the advancing tide of humanity will come with its flocks and herds, and the ancient silence and desolation will be no more; and this thought is like human companionship, and mitigates the effect of nature's wildness on the spirit. In Patagonia no such thought or dream of the approaching changes to be wrought by human agency can affect the mind. There is no water there, the arid soil is sand and gravel—pebbles rounded by the action of ancient seas, before Europe was; and nothing grows except the barren things that nature loves—thorns, and a few woody herbs, and scattered tufts of wiry bitter grass.

Doubtless we are not all affected in solitude by wild nature in the same degree; even in the Patagonian wastes many would probably experience no such mental change as I have described. Others have their instincts nearer to the surface, and are moved deeply by nature in any solitary place; and I imagine that Thoreau was such a one. At all events, although he was without the Darwinian lights which we have, and these feelings were always to him "strange," "mysterious," "unaccountable," he does not conceal them. This is the "something uncanny in Thoreau" which seems inexplicable and startling to such as have never been startled by nature, nor deeply moved; but which, to others, imparts a peculiarly delightful aromatic flavour to his writings. It is his wish towards a more primitive mode of life, his strange abandonment when he scours the wood like a half-starved hound, and no morsel could be too savage for him; the desire to take a ranker hold on life and live more as the animals do; the sympathy with nature so keen that it takes his breath away; the feeling that all the elements were congenial to him, which made the wildest scenes unaccountably familiar, so that he came and went with a strange liberty in nature. Once only he had doubts, and thought that human companionship might be essential to happiness; but he was at the same time conscious of a slight insanity in the mood; and he soon again became sensible of the sweet beneficent society of nature, of an infinite and unaccountable friendliness all at once like an atmosphere sustaining him. In the limits of a chapter it is impossible to do more than touch the surface of so large a subject as that of the instincts and remains of instincts existing in us. Dr. Wallace doubts that there are any human instincts, even in the perfect savage; which seems strange in so keen an observer, and one who has lived so much with nature and uncivilized men; but it must be borne in mind that his peculiar theories with regard to man's origin—the acquisition of large brains, naked body, and the upright form not through but in spite of natural selection—would predispose him to take such a view. My own experience and observation have led me to a contrary conclusion, and my belief is that we might learn something by looking more beneath the hardened crust of custom into the still burning core. For instance, that experience I had in Patagonia—the novel state of mind I have described—seemed to furnish an answer to a question frequently asked with regard to men living in a state of nature. When we consider that our intellect, unlike that of the inferior animals, is progressive, how wonderful it seems that communities and tribes of men should exist—"are contented to exist," we often say, just as if they had any choice in the matter—for ages and for thousands of years in a state of pure barbarism, living from hand to mouth, exposed to extremes of temperature, and to frequently-recurring famine even in the midst of the greatest fertility, when a little foresight—"the smallest amount of intelligence possessed by the lowest of mankind," we say—would be sufficient to make their condition immeasurably better. If, in the wild natural life, their normal state is like that into which I temporarily fell, then it no longer appears strange to me that they take no thought for the morrow, and remain stationary, and are only a little removed from other mammalians, their superiority in this respect being only sufficient to counterbalance their physical disadvantages. That instinctive state of the human mind, when the higher faculties appear to be non-existent, a state of intense alertness and preparedness, which compels the man to watch and listen and go silently and stealthily, must be like that of the lower animals: the brain is then like a highly-polished mirror, in which all visible nature—every hill, tree, leaf—is reflected with miraculous clearness; and we can imagine that if the animal could think and reason, thought would be superfluous and a hindrance, since it would dim that bright perception on which his safety depends.

That is a part, the lesser part, of the lesson I learnt in the Patagonian solitude: the second larger part must be cut very short; for on all sides it leads to other questions, some of which would probably be thought "more curious than edifying." That hidden fiery core is nearer to us than we ordinarily imagine, and its heat still permeates the crust to keep us warm. This is, no doubt, a matter of annoyance and even grief to those who grow impatient at Nature's unconscionable slowness; who wish to be altogether independent of such an underlying brute energy; to live on a cool crust and rapidly grow angelic. But, as things are, it is, perhaps, better to be still, for a while, a little lower than the angels: we are hardly in a position just yet to dispense with the unangelic qualities, even in this exceedingly complex state, in which we appear to be so effectually "hedged in from harm." I recall here an incident witnessed by a friend of mine of an Indian he and his fellow-soldiers were pursuing who might easily have escaped unharmed; but when his one companion was thrown to the ground through his horse falling, the first Indian turned deliberately, sprang to the earth, and, standing motionless by the other's side, received the white men's bullets. Not for love—it would be absurd to suppose such a thing—but inspired by that fierce instinctive spirit of defiance which in some cases will actually cause a man to go out of his way to seek death. Why are we, children of light—the light which makes us timid—so strongly stirred by a deed like this, so useless and irrational, and feel an admiration so great that compared with it that which is called forth by the noblest virtue, or the highest achievement of the intellect, seems like a pale dim feeling? It is because in our inmost natures, our deepest feelings, we are still one with the savage. We admire a Gordon less for his godlike qualities—his spirituality, and crystal purity of heart, and justice, and love of his kind—than for that more ancient nobility, the qualities he had in common with the wild man of childish intellect, an old Viking, a fighting Colonel Burnaby, a Captain Webb who madly flings his life away, a vulgar Welsh prize fighter who enters a den full of growling lions, and drives them before him like frightened sheep. It is due to this instinctive savage spirit in us, in spite of our artificial life and all we have done to rid ourselves of an inconvenient heritage, that we are capable of so-called heroic deeds; of cheerfully exposing ourselves to the greatest privations and hardships, suffering them stoically, and facing death without blenching, sacrificing our lives, as we say, in the cause of humanity, or geography, or some other branch of science.

It is related that a late aged prime minister of England on one occasion stood for several hours at his sovereign's side at a reception, in an oppressive atmosphere, and suffering excruciating pains from a gouty foot; yet making no sign and concealing his anguish under a smiling countenance. We have been told that this showed his good blood, that because he came of a good stock, and had the training and traditional feelings of a gentleman, he was able to suffer in that calm way. This pretty delusion quickly vanishes in a surgical hospital, or on a field covered with wounded men after a fight. But the savage always endures pain more stoically than the civilized man. He is

> Self-balanced against contingencies,
> As the trees and animals are.

However great the sufferings of the gouty premier may have been, they were less than those which any Indian youth in Guiana and Venezuela voluntarily subjects himself to before he ventures to call himself a man, or to ask for a wife. Small in comparison, yet he did not endure them smilingly because the traditional pride and other feelings of a gentleman made it possible for him to do so, but because that more ancient and nobler pride, the stern instinct of endurance of the savage, came to his aid and sustained him.

These things do not, or at all events should not, surprise us. They can only surprise those who are without the virile instinct, or who have never become conscious of it on account of the circumstances of their lives. The only wonder is that the stern indomitable spirit in us should ever in any circumstances fail a man, that even on the scaffold or with the world against him he should be overcome by despair, and burst into weak tears and lamentations, and faint in the presence of his fellows. In one of the most eloquent passages of his finest work Herman Melville describes as follows that manly spirit or instinct in us, and the effect produced on us by the sight of its failure: "Men may seem detestable as joint-stock companies and nations; knaves, fools, and murderers there may be; men may have mean and meagre faces; but man, in the ideal, is so noble and so sparkling, such a grand and glowing creature, that over any ignominious blemish in him all his fellows should run to throw their costliest robes. That immaculate manliness we feel in ourselves—so far within us that it remains intact though all the outer character seems gone—bleeds with keenest anguish at the spectacle of a valour-ruined man. Nor can piety itself, at such a shameful sight, completely stifle her upbraidings against the permitting stars. But this august dignity I treat of, is not the dignity of kings and robes, but the abounding dignity which has no robed investiture. Thou shalt see it shining in the arm that wields a pick and drives a spike; that democratic dignity which, on all hands, radiates without end from God Himself."

There is then something to be said in favour of this animal and primitive nature in us. Thoreau, albeit so spiritually-minded, could yet "reverence" that lower nature in him which made him brother to the brute. He experienced and fully appreciated its tonic effect. And until we get a better civilization more equal in its ameliorating effect on all classes—if there must be classes—and more likely to endure, it is perhaps a fortunate thing that we have so far failed to eliminate the "savage" in us—the "Old Man" as some might prefer to call it. Not a respectable Old Man, but a very useful one occasionally, when we stand in sore need of his services and he comes promptly and unsummoned to our aid.

1. In an article on "Courage," by Lord Wolseley, in the *Fortnightly Review* for August 1889, there occurs the following passage, descriptive of the state of mind experienced by men in fight: "All maddening pleasures seem to be compressed into that very short space of time, and yet every sensation experienced in those fleeting moments is so indelibly impressed on the brain that not even the most trifling incident is ever forgotten in after life."

XIV

THE PERFUME OF AN EVENING PRIMROSE

I SOMETIMES walk in a large garden where the evening primrose is permitted to grow, but only at the extreme end of the ground, thrust away, as it were, back against the unkept edge with its pretty tangle of thorn, briar, and woodbine, to keep company there with a few straggling poppies, with hollyhook, red and white foxglove, and other coarse and weed-like plants, all together forming a kind of horizon, dappled with colour, to the garden on that side, a suitable background to the delicate more valued blooms. It has a neglected appearance, its tall straggling stems insufficiently clothed with leaves, leaning away from contact with the hedge; a plant of somewhat melancholy aspect, suggesting to a fanciful mind the image of a maiden originally intended by Nature to be her most perfect type of grace and ethereal loveliness, but who soon outgrew her strength with all beauty of form, and who now wanders abroad, careless of appearances, in a faded flimsy garment, her fair yellow hair dishevelled, her mournful eyes fixed ever on the earth where she will shortly be.

I never pass this weedy, pale-flowered alien without stooping to thrust my nose into first one blossom then another, and still another, until that organ, like some industrious bee, is thickly powered with the golden dust. If, after an interval, I find myself once more at the same spot, I repeat this performance with as much care as if it was a kind of religious ceremony it would not be safe to omit; and at all times I am as reluctant to pass without approaching my nose to it, as the great Dr. Johnson was to pass a street-post without touching it with his hand. My motive, however, is not a superstitious one, nor is it merely one of those meaningless habits which men sometimes contract, and of which they are scarcely conscious. When I first knew the evening primrose, where it is both a wild and a garden flower and very common, I did not often smell at it, but was satisfied to inhale its subtle fragrance from the air. And this reminds me that

EVENING PRIMROSE

in England it does not perfume the air as it certainly does on the pampas of La Plata, in the early morning in places where it is abundant; here its fragrance, while unchanged in character, has either become less volatile or so diminished in quantity that one is not sensible that the flower possesses a perfume until he approaches his nose to it.

My sole motive in smelling the evening primrose is the pleasure it gives me. This pleasure greatly surpasses that which I receive from other flowers far more famous for their fragrance, for it is in a great degree mental, and is due to association. Why is this pleasure so vivid, so immeasurably greater than the mental pleasure afforded by the sight of the flower? The books tell us that sight, the most important of our senses, is the most intellectual; while smell, the least important, is in man the most emotional sense. This is a very brief statement of the fact; I will now restate it another way and more fully.

I am now holding an evening primrose in my hand. As a fact at this moment I am holding nothing but the pen with which I am writing this chapter; but I am supposing myself back in the garden, and holding the flower that first suggested this train of thought. I turn it about this way and that, and although it pleases it does not delight, does not move me: certainly I do not think very highly of its beauty, although it is beautiful; placed beside the rose, the fuchsia, the azalea, or the lily, it would not attract the eye. But it is a link with the past, it summons vanished scenes to my mind. I recognize that the plant I plucked it from possesses a good deal of adaptiveness, a quality one would scarcely suspect from seeing it only in an English garden. Thus I remember that I first knew it as a garden flower, that it grew large, on a large plant, as here; that on summer evenings I was accustomed to watch its slim, pale, yellow buds unfold, and called it, when speaking in Spanish, by its quaint native name of *James of the night*, and, in English, primrose simply. I recall with a smile that it was a shock to my childish mind to learn that our primrose was not *the* primrose. Then, I remember, came the time when I could ride out over the plain; and it surprised me to discover that this primrose, unlike the four-o'clock and morning-glory, and other evening flowers in our garden, was also a wild flower. I knew it by its unmistakable perfume, but on those plains, where the grass was cropped close, the plant was small, only a few inches high, and the flowers no bigger than buttercups. Afterwards I met with it again in the swampy woods and everglades along the Plata River; and there it grew tall and rank, five or six feet high in some cases, with large flowers that had only a faint perfume. Still later, going on longer expeditions, sometimes with cattle, I found it in extraordinary abundance on the level pampas south of the Salado River; there it was a tall slender plant, grass-like among the tall grasses, with wide open flowers about an inch in diameter, and not more than two or three on each plant. Finally, I remember that on first landing in Patagonia, on a desert part of the coast, the time being a little after daybreak, I became conscious of the familiar perfume in the air, and, looking about me, discovered a plant growing on the barren sand not many yards from the sea; there it grew, low and bush-like in form, with stiff horizontal stems and a profusion of small symmetrical flowers.

All this about the plant, and much more, with many scenes and events of the past, are suggested to my mind, by the flower in my hand; but while these scenes and events are recalled with pleasure it is a kind of mental pleasure that we frequently experience, and very slight in degree. But when I approach the flower to my face and inhale its perfume, then a shock of keen pleasure is experienced, and a mental change so great that it is like a miracle. For a space of time so short that if it could be measured it would probably be found to occupy no more than a fraction of a second, I am no longer in an English garden recalling and consciously thinking about that vanished past, but during that brief moment time and space seem annihilated and the past is now. I am again on the grassy pampas, where I have been sleeping very soundly under the stars—would that I could now sleep as soundly under a roof! It is the moment of wakening, when my eyes are just opening to the pure over-arching sky, flushed in its eastern half with tender colour; and at the moment that nature thus reveals itself to my vision in its exquisite morning beauty and freshness, I am sensible of the subtle primrose perfume in the air. The blossoms are all about me, for miles and for leagues on that great level expanse, as if the morning wind had blown them out of that eastern sky and scattered their pale yellow stars in millions over the surface of the tall sere grass.

I do not say that this shock of pleasure I have described, this vivid reproduction of a long past scene, is experienced each time I smell the flower; it is experienced fully only at long intervals, after weeks and months, when the fragrance is, so to speak, new to me, and afterwards in a lesser degree on each repetition, until the feeling is exhausted. If I continue to smell again and again at the flower, I do it only as a spur to memory; or in mechanical way, just person might always walk along a certain path with his eyes fixed on the ground, remembering that he once on a time dropped some valuable article there, and although he knows that it was lost irrecoverably, he still searches the ground for it.

Other vegetable odours affect me in a similar way, but in a very much fainter degree, except in one or two cases. Thus, the Lombardy poplar was one of the trees I first became acquainted with in childhood, and it has ever since been a pleasure to me to see it; but in spring, when its newly opened leaves give out their peculiar aroma, for a moment, when I first smell it, I am actually a boy again, among the tall poplar trees, their myriads of heart-shaped leaves rustling to the hot November wind, and sparkling like silver in the brilliant sunshine. More than that, I am, in that visionary moment, clinging fast to the slim vertical branches, high above the earth, forty or fifty feet perhaps; and just where I have ceased from climbing, in the cleft of a branch and against the white bark, I see the dainty little cup-shaped nest I have been seeking; and round my head, as I gaze down in it, delighted at the sight of the small pearly eggs it contains, flutter the black-headed, golden-winged siskins, uttering their long canary-like notes of solicitude. It all comes and goes like a flash of lightning, but the scene revealed, and the accompanying feeling, the complete recovery of a lost sensation, are wonderfully real. Nothing that we see or hear can thus restore the past. The sight of the poplar tree, the sound made by the wind in its summer foliage, the song of the golden-winged siskins when I meet with them in captivity, bring up many past scenes to my mind, and among others the picture I have described; but it is a picture only, until the fragrance of the poplar touches the nerve of smell, and then it is something more.

I have no doubt that my experience is similar to that of others, especially of those who have lived a rural life, and whose senses have been trained by an early-acquired habit of attention. When we read of Cuvier (and the same thing has been recorded of others), that the scent of some humble flower or weed, familiar to him in boyhood, would always affect him to tears, I presume that the poignant feeling of grief—grief, that is, for the loss of a vanished happiness—which ended in tears, succeeded to some such vivid representation of the past as I have described, and to the purely delightful recovery of a vanished sensation. Not only flowery and aromatic odours can produce this powerful effect; it is caused by any smell, not positively disagreeable, which may be in any way associated with a happy period in early or past life: the smell, for instance, of peat smoke, of a brewery, a tan yard, of cattle and sheep, and sheep-folds, of burning weeds, brushwood, and charcoal; the dank smell of marshes, and the smell, "ancient and fish-like," that clings about many seaside towns and villages; also the smell of the sea itself, and of decaying seaweed, and the dusty smell of rain in summer, and the smell of new mown hay, and of stables and of freshly-ploughed ground, with so many others that every reader can add to the list from his own experience. Being so common a thing, it may be thought that I have dwelt too long on it. My excuse must be that some things are common without being familiar; also that some common things have not yet been explained.

Locke somewhere says that unless we refresh our mental pictures of what we have seen by looking again at their originals, they fade, and in the end are lost. Bain appears to have the same opinion, at all events he says: "The simplest impression that can be made, of taste, smell, touch, hearing, sight, needs repetition in order to endure of its own accord." Probably it is a fact that when any scene, not yet lost by the memory, a house, let us say, is looked at again after a long interval, it does not, unless seen in a new setting, create a new image distinct from the old and faded one, but covers the former image, so to speak, the pre-existent picture, and may therefore be said to freshen it. Most of the impressions we receive are no doubt very transitory, but it is certainly an error that all our mental pictures, not freshened in the way described, fade and disappear, since it is in the experience of every one of us that many mental pictures of scenes looked at once only, and in some cases only for a few moments, remain persistently in the mind. But the remembered scenes or objects do not present themselves to the mental eye perfect and in their first vivid colours, except on very rare occasions; they are like certain old paintings that always look dark and obscured until a wet sponge is passed over them, whereupon for a short time they recover their clearness of outline and brilliancy of colour. In recalling the past, emotion plays the part of the wet sponge, and it is excited most powerfully in us when we encounter, after a long interval, some once familiar odour associated in some way with the picture recalled. But why? Not finding an answer in the books, I am compelled to seek for one, true or false, in the wilderness of my own mind.

The reason, I imagine, is that while smells are so much to us they cannot, like things seen and things heard, be reproduced in the mind, but are at once forgotten. It is true that in the books smell is classified along with taste, as being much lower or less intellectual than sight and hearing, for the reason (scarcely a valid one) that there must be actual contact of the organ of smell with the object smelt, or a material emanation from, and portion of, such object, although the object itself might be miles away beyond the sight or even beyond the horizon. The light of nature is enough to show how false the arrangement is that places smell and taste together, as much lower and widely apart from sight and hearing. Rather the extreme delicacy of the olfactory nerve raises smell to the rank of an intellectual sense, but very little below the two first and higher senses. And yet, while sights and sounds are retained and can be reproduced at will, and their phantasms are like the reality, an odour has no phantasm in the brain; or, to be very exact, the phantasm of an odour, or its presentment, or representation, is so faint and quickly gone when any effort is made to recover it, that, compared with the distinct and abiding presentments of sights and sounds, it is as nothing. Imagine, for example, that you had often seen Windsor Castle, and knew a great deal about it, its history, its noble appearance, which will look familiar to you when you see it again and affect you pleasantly as in the past; and that yet you could not see it with the mind's eye, but that when, after a recent visit, you tried to see it mentally, nothing but a formless, dim, whitish patch appeared, only to disappear in an instant and come no more. Such a case would represent our condition with regard to even the strongest and most familiar smells. Yet in spite of our inability to recall them, we do distinctly make the effort; and in the case of some strong odour which we have recently inhaled, the mind mocks us with this faint shadow of a phantasm; and this vain, or almost vain, effort of the mind seems to show that odours in some past period of our history were so much more to us than they are now that they could be vividly reproduced, and that this power has been lost, or, at all events, is so weakened as to be of no use.

I find that Bain, who makes different and contradictory statements on this subject in his work on *The Senses and the Intellect*, has the following sentence, with which I agree: "By a great effort of the mind, we may approach very near to the recovery of a smell that we have been extremely familiar with, as, for example, the odour of coffee, and if we were more dependent on ideas of smell, we might succeed much better." A very big *if*, by the way; but it is probable that some savages, and some individuals among us that have a very acute sense of smell, do succeed much better. This sense being so much more to dogs than to man, it is not strange that they remember smells rather than sights, and can reproduce the sensation of smells, as their twitching and sniffing noses when they dream seem to show.

This approach in ourselves to the recovery of a strong or familiar smell, this dim white patch, to speak in metaphor, the ghost of a phantasm of a smell, seems to have misled the philosophers into the idea that we can mentally reproduce odours. Bain, as I have said, contradicts himself, and therefore, excepting in the sentence I have quoted, must be put down among those who are against me; and with him are McCosh, Bastian, Luys, Ferrier, and others who write on the brain and the mind. Do they copy from each other? It is very odd that they all tell us that we know very little about the sense of smell, and prove it by affirming that we can recall the sensations produced by odours, in some cases quoting the poet:

Odours, when sweet violets sicken,
Live within the sense they quicken.

I was seriously alarmed at the beginning of this inquiry by reading in McCosh: "When the organs of taste and smell, supposed by Ferrier to be at the back of the head, are diseased or out of order, the reproduction of the corresponding sensations may be indistinct." So indistinct was the reproduction in my own case, even of the smell of coffee, that after reading this passage I began to fear that my own brain had misled me, and so, to satisfy myself on the point, I consulted others, friends and acquaintances, who all began trying to recall the sensations produced on them by the odours they were most familiar with. The result of their efforts has restored my peace of mind. With the exception of two or three ladies, who, having no male relations to make up their minds for them, profess to be still in doubt, all sadly acknowledged that they find themselves poorer by one faculty than they had supposed themselves to be; that they began trying to recall smells in the belief that they had the power; that they found that they could almost do it, then began to doubt, and finally with a feeling of impotence, of being baffled, gave it up.

A simple mental experiment may serve to convince any person who tries it that the sensations of smell do not reproduce themselves in the mind. We think of a rose, or a lily, or a violet, and a feeling of pleasure attends the thought; but that this feeling is caused solely by the image of something beautiful to the eye becomes evident when we proceed to think of some artificial perfume, or extract, or essence of a flower. The extract, we know, gave us far more pleasure than the slight perfume of the flower, but there is no feeling of pleasure in thinking of it: it is nothing more than an idea in the mind. On the other hand, when we remember some extremely painful scene that we have witnessed, or some sound, expressing distress or anguish, that we have heard, something of the distressed feeling experienced at the time is reproduced in us; and it is common to hear people say, It makes me sad, or makes me dizzy, or makes my blood run cold, when I think of it; which is literally true, because in thinking of it they again (in a sense) see and hear it. But to think of evil odours does not affect us at all: we can, in imagination, uncork and sniff at cans of petroleum and saturate our pocket-handkerchiefs with asafœtida or carbolic acid, or walk behind a dust-cart, or wade through miles of fetid slime in some tropical morass, or take up some mephitic animal, like the skunk, and fondle it as we would a kitten, yet experience no pain, and no sensation of nausea. We can, if we like, call up all the sweet and abominable smells in nature, just as Owen Glendower called spirits from the vasty deep, but, like the spirits, they refuse to come; or they come not as smells but as ideas, so that phosphuretted hydrogen causes no pain, and frangipane no pleasure. We only know that smells exist; that we have roughly classified them as fragrant, aromatic, fresh, ethereal, stimulating, acrid, nauseous, and virulent; that each of these generic names includes a very large number of distinct odours: we know them all because the mind has taken note of the distinct character of each, and of its effect on us, not because it has registered a sensation in our brain to be reproduced at will, as in the case of something we have seen or heard.

It is true that we are equally powerless to recall tastes. Bain admits that "these sensations are deficient as regards the power of being remembered"; but he did not discover the fact himself, nor does he verify it from his own experience, merely telling us that "Longet observes." But taste is not an emotional sense. I know, for instance, that if I were to partake of some once familiar, long untasted dish, flavoured, let me say, with some such abomination (to the English palate) as cummin-seed or garlic; some vegetable, or fruit, wild or cultivated, that I never see in England, it would not move me as I am moved by an odour, and would perhaps give me less pleasure than a dish of strawberries and cream. For in the flavour there is obvious contact with the organ of taste; it is gross and inseparable from the thing eaten to supply a bodily want, and gives a momentary and purely animal gratification; therefore to the mind it is not in the same category, but very much lower than that invisible, immaterial something that flies to us, not to give a sensuous pleasure only, but also to lead, to warn, to instruct, and call up before the mental eye bright images of things unseen. Consequently our inability to recall past flavours is not felt as a loss, and no effort is made to recover them; they are lost and were not worth keeping.

This, then, to my mind, is the reason that smell is an emotional sense in so great a degree, compared with the other senses—namely, because, like sight and hearing, it is an intellectual sense, and because, unlike sight and hearing, its sensations are forgotten; and when after a long interval a forgotten odour, once familiar and associated intimately with the past, is again encountered, the sudden, unexpected recovery of a lost sensation affects us in some such way as the accidental discovery of a store of gold, hidden away by ourselves in some past period of our life and forgotten; or as it would affect us to be met face to face by some dear friend, long absent and supposed to be dead. The suddenly recovered sensation is more to us for a moment than a mere sensation; it is like a recovery of the irrecoverable past. We are not moved in this way, or at all events not nearly in the same degree, by seeing objects or hearing sounds that are associated with and recall past scenes, simply because the old familiar sights and sounds have never been forgotten; their phantasms have always existed in the brain. If, for instance, I hear a bird's note that I have not heard for the last twenty years, it is not as if I had not really heard it, since I have listened to it mentally a thousand times during the interval, and it does not surprise or come to me like something that was lost and is recovered, and consequently does not move me. And so with the sensation of sight; I cannot think of any fragrant flower that glows in my distant home without seeing it, so that its beauty may always be enjoyed;—but its fragrance, alas, has vanished and returns not!

WAKENING AT DAWN

INDEX

Also Available from Nonsuch Publishing

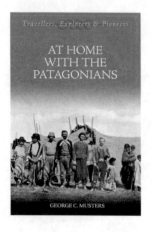

In 1869-70 George C. Musters spent a year living with the nomadic tribes of the Tehuelche in Patagonia. *At Home with the Patagonians* is a fascinating insight into a people and way of life so far removed from modern civilisation, yet in many ways remarkably similar.
£14
ISBN: 1-84588-008-0
256 pages, 10 illustrations

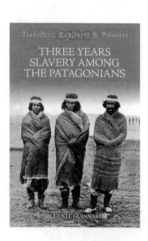

At the age of just 23 Auguste Guinnard was captured by Patagonian Indians and forced to live and work with them as their slave. *Three Years' Slavery* is a faithful record of Guinnard's brutal enslavement, surprising enlightenment and eventual escape and return to his homeland.
£12
ISBN: 1-84588-046-3
160 pages

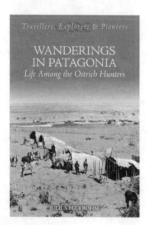

Setting out on what should have been a simple journey from Port Julian to Sandy Point the author and his companions find themselves facing unexpected dangers, from raging rivers to mutineers, in an adventure that turns out to be anything but simple.
£12
ISBN: 1-84588-062-5
160 pages, 9 illustrations